I MADE IT OUT

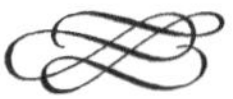

AVISHAI EL

BEATRICE PRESS

COPYRIGHT

ISBN EBOOK: 9798985100808

ISBN PAPERBACK: 9798985100815

Publisher

CONTENTS

Foreword   v

Chapter 1   1
Chapter 2   20
Chapter 3   40
Chapter 4   61
Chapter 5   76
Chapter 6   97
Chapter 7   115
Chapter 8   134

Places   155
About the Author   157
Also by Avishai El   159

FOREWORD

Avishai El's book, I Made It Out, is a sincerely candid and truthful account of her experiences thus far in her life. I have known Avishai for all of her life and I can corroborate all of the experiences which I have been privy to. I Made It Out will take you along a winding road journey of love and laughter, joy and pain, trauma and heart break, conquest and success. This book is an exemplary display of Avishai's resounding strength and amazing resilience as well as her tenacious ability to fight the good fight and never give up. Throughout her entire life, there has been one challenge after another. She has from a very young age, experienced traumas that no child should ever be exposed to.

Avishai will share these distressing life-altering events with her readers as well as share how these events were instrumental in helping to shape and build her character. She is such a wonderfully gifted and multi-faceted person with so many talents in which she has exhibited and incorporated in this autobiography. Even though she's been through numerous trials and adversities, one of her greatest gifts is the incredible ability to bring light and laughter to those who have suffered through darkness and tears. I should know because I'm her mother and I am extremely elated with joy and happiness to be able to witness the progressive evolution of my beautiful daughter, Avishai.

I sincerely love you,
    Sahar El

CHAPTER 1

My birth may have been planned, the date of July 11th, 1989, my expected date, but my size certainly was not. I am told I was beautiful – brown skin, black curly hair, chubby cheeks, full lips, slanted eyes, and weighing 11lbs 11ozs. My mother, Sahar El dispatched my father, Michael Pullam, to buy more clothes as there was no way any of the ones gifted at my mom's baby shower would fit. My father, a former marine, had settled with my mother in Newington, Connecticut in my childhood home on Willard Avenue.

On leaving the marines my father worked as a psych aid supporting patients with mental health issues. My mom was a software engineer at an insurance company. She was always a beautiful woman and I loved looking at her light eyes and high cheekbones. My father was handsome with a prominent mustache, which would prick me when he would pick me up and kiss me. Unfortunately, alcoholism and chain-smoking cigarettes was a struggle for my father. I can still smell his scent, a mix of beer and cigarettes, until this day.

When my mom worked, he would stay home and watch me. I was a daddy's girl. He was my best friend and someone that I thought I would be close to forever. He was a good father, filled with love and compassion for his daughter. Sleeping was not my strong suit as a baby, so he would drive me around in his car until I fell asleep. Although I was a baby, I still remember how good I felt and how the sky looked. The purple skies passing away into a midnight blue as the sun was saying, 'goodbye.'

Who would have thought that the sun's 'goodbye' would be an omen for my life? Who knew the person that I was the closest to would turn into a stranger?

Then came the day I will never forget. I was one year old. Riding in the car with my father was the norm, but this day was different. This time he was not driving me around so I could fall asleep. He had other plans. If I could title this day, it would be, 'Abandoned Betrayal'. We arrived at a family member's house, but one of us would stay, and the other leave.

I don't remember the conversation between the person in that house and my father, but I still remember the terror of being in her room in a car seat, feeling lost, and abandoned. The man who watched me every single day had left and never came back. It turns out my father had been cheating on my mom and that same year she filed for divorce. My mom remained single, but my father found himself a new family and even adopted those children as his own. I did not see him often.

After the divorce my father started to act different. He didn't want to come visit me at my mom's house. When I was two and a half years old it was court ordered that my mom bring me to my paternal grandmother's house for visitation. Although my mom was told that my father would see me at his mom's house, she was reluctant to take me there. Very protective of me she never let me spend the night with relatives, so this was a huge change for her. However, she had to follow the court order so she would take me over there every other Friday. I remember my paternal grandmother was not affectionate. For example, when she held my hand, she would grip it so tightly it hurt. The woman was rigid in her everyday routine and was never one to express love or say she loved me, so I couldn't tell whether she did, or she didn't. The poor excuse of a man she was married to would soon be exposed as a vicious predator who pretended to be kind. What was supposed to be a joyous time with my father would later turn into years of trauma healing. Every other Friday my mom dropped me off and I was always met by my paternal grandmother. She was the epitome of how a stereotypical evil witch looked. Her energy was never pleasant or welcoming and she was emotionally cold. She and my mom would walk me in. When my mom left my father would come for a few minutes and then leave.

On rare occasions he would take me somewhere. The only time I remember him actually spending time with me at that age was when he went to get himself a sandwich filled with sprouts. He let me have a bite of his sandwich but didn't get me a sandwich. I always thought that was the weirdest thing to do. If I had a child, I would have also bought them something to eat. My father was a detached individual who acted impulsively. He was someone who would leave people, such as my mom and I, filled with unanswered questions. For example, him leaving was an impulsive action. There was no explanation. Another example is the time I asked my father about nationality. I asked my father, "What is my nationality?" His response, "We're everything." In my estimation his actions didn't make sense to me. He wasn't the type to admit to anything or take accountability. Saying, "Sorry" was not a part of his vocabulary and he always appeared aloof. This aloof, detached attitude that my father possessed put my life in danger. What was seen as 'doing the right thing' by my mom, because she followed a court order and didn't want to keep her daughter away from her father, would later bring immense pain and sadness.

Every other Friday when I went to see my father at my paternal grandmother's house, my mom would check in and my grandmother would make it seem as if she was there watching me at all times and would tell my mom that my father came over. My paternal grandmother would tell my mom I was doing fine. The reality was, unbeknown to my mom I wasn't left with my father or his mother, I was left with my paternal grandmother's husband. He was an elderly man who I saw as a monster. That creature from hell looked like a classic Mr. Rogers to the average person. He would even smile at other people so you wouldn't suspect the evil lurking underneath that mild exterior. He was very deceptive.

Every time I went over there, I was terrified, but I didn't say a word to my mom. He abused me sexually and made me do despicable things against my will. He cussed often and called me a bitch. When I was left alone with him, he displayed different personalities. I saw a warped individual, not a person. I was only two-and-a-half to three-years old when I was violently abused.

No child should have to be brutalized. I remember wanting to run away from the house but he blocked me from leaving. I felt trapped. I can recall my mom dropping me off with another family member in the car. My paternal grandmother was outside to walk me in. I cried uncontrollably and was petrified to enter that house. The look on my mom's face was one of uncertainty. She looked as though she didn't want to leave me and kept asking me if I wanted to come with her. My maternal grandmother who was in the car with her said, "Just go 'head," an irritated edge to her voice. My paternal grandmother would say, "Let's go in. She's going to be fine. We're going to go get breakfast." This put my mother's fears at ease. Yet, once again, she lied to my mom. She ended up leaving me with that monster again and then came the worst day of all. I had no clothes on, as usual, when I was around him and I could feel something sharp poking me in my rectal area. It felt like a knife and/or something sharp pulling at that opening. All I remember this evil son of a bitch saying was, "Oh shit." I couldn't take it anymore being over there. I had, had enough of being at that house.

During this incident I spoke quietly to myself and said, "I can't take it anymore." I got tired of being abused physically, sexually, and verbally. Every part of me was invaded every other week. My sleep was even interrupted because to the best of my recollection he would come into the room. Once my paternal grandmother caught him. Instead of saying something to him she got a belt and threatened to hit me with it. I thought she was super evil. They were perfect for each other. She knew about the abuse and did nothing about it. I felt as though I was being held hostage every other week and now looking back, I really was. I couldn't have fun. I was treated like a sex slave and an object that had no voice.

The last time I went over there was when that incident occurred. I still remember this day as if it was yesterday. It was nighttime and my mom came to pick me up. I didn't say a word the entire ride. I was in complete shock. Yes, my body had been violated multiple times, but that day was different. I was too young to know anything about spirituality, but I knew that if I continued to go over there I would be pushed over the edge. I may have lost my mind and had even more severe psychological issues. From what my mom tells me, I told her the next day. My mom was giving me a bath and saw I was bleeding. She called the doctor and also a family member.

This family member was watching me prior to me going over my paternal grandmother's house. She got a new job so she couldn't watch me anymore, but she was so peaceful and pleasant when she babysat. She never yelled at me or hit me. When my mom called my family member, she told her to ask me if anybody touched me.

That's when I told my mom, 'Monster' did it. Once I told her she took me to several doctors, including my pediatrician. The doctor I normally went to as a baby saw evidence of abuse and the doctor at Saint Francis Hospital found evidence of abuse and trauma. The evidence from those visits showed that there was bruising and trauma in my vaginal area.

Once there was evidence my mom filed a report to have 'Monster' thrown in jail. After that I had to go see a child psychologist. It was recommended that I go to him for psychological treatment. He confirmed that I was telling the truth about what 'Monster' had done to me. When I was finished with psychiatric treatment the doctor asked my mom, "Are you going to press charges?"

That was when she contacted a couple police stations until someone was willing to help her. The investigating officer dragged the case out. Different people were put on the cases and didn't do their job properly. The captain said they didn't have enough evidence to bring it to trial and closed the case.

My mom wrote a letter to the Chief of Police, and he referred the case to a sergeant. She told them everything that happened, and they reopened the case. The case moved forward. I spoke to the prosecutor on several occasions and the case went to trial. 'Monster' pleaded no contest and got nine months in prison after three long years of fighting to have him convicted.

I was six years old when he went to jail. My mom made sure he went to jail and went through this process alone. She had some family support from a very small group of people. Emotions were running high when 'Monster' went to jail and some people , already in prison, said they were going to kill him when he arrived. A stop was put to it and he was released after nine months.

I continued with my life a bit happier than before. When I first started the psychiatric sessions, you could visibly see in photographs that I was traumatized and very sad. Once I finished those sessions at four years old, I started to smile again. When I turned five kindergarten was the next chapter in my life.

My mom had prepared me for kindergarten by teaching me how to read when I was three years old. This was our bonding time. We would read my favorite books, *Corduroy, Ruby To The Rescue,* and *Peter's Chair.* She would read the story and every time she would get to words like, a, the, or and, I would say those along with her.

After that I started sounding words out. My mom made sure I knew my numbers, colors, and everything else so that when I started kindergarten, I felt confident and did my best.

On my first day of kindergarten, I was excited. My mom had dressed me in green corduroy shorts, a white turtleneck, and a vest that was half green and half floral. I wore glasses with purple rims and fictitious animated characters on them. My prescription was very strong. I couldn't see a thing without glasses. Everything and everyone looked like a blob. My hair was half up, half down, and shoulder length. My maternal grandmother had straightened my hair with a hot comb because my hair was naturally curly, and I wanted it straight. I loved my hair and looked forward to going to school. My mom was nervous the entire morning. I couldn't tell she was until she told me years later. However, I was filled with nothing, but excitement. She took me to an elementary school at Newington, Connecticut. All the children had to line up with their teachers and classmates. I can recall turning around, looking at my mom, and telling her that she could leave and go to work. She was going to wait, but I was fine, so she felt comfortable leaving

My teacher was a very kind woman. She was short with a long, pointed face, brown curly hair, and brown eyes. Her voice was soft and soothing, which was suitable for small children. I always looked forward to sitting on the carpet as she read books. I loved the way she turned the pages. She had a very comforting demeanor and was quietly protective of her students. She would hold our hands from time to time and sit us on her lap. I loved that she had a close eye on us and felt protected in her presence. My favorite memories of kindergarten were when we painted in class and had to mix colors of paints to create a new one.

I also loved when she would ask us what kind of milk we wanted. Milk was comforting to me for whatever reason. When we had independent and partner reading, she would offer us these huge soda crackers. Those were my favorite crackers. She was the best teacher and the only elementary teacher who recognized me as a special student. I was the top reader in her kindergarten class, and she gave me an award for reading. I helped other students with their reading in the class and felt overjoyed. She treated me like a leader, and it was empowering. There were girls in my class who were popular, not melanated like me, and spoiled.

Most of these children had two parents that gave them everything. I didn't really fit in with them, but it didn't make me feel less than them. I had confidence in who I was as a melanated child because of how I was raised. I never wanted to look like the other children. I would sometimes punch some of these girls out of anger. The anger definitely stemmed from the trauma I had experienced a couple years back. I recall punching one of the girls in the stomach. Other times I would blackout and not remember what happened. What I did remember was my teacher calling the girl's mom and my mom to talk about the ordeal. My teacher was very calm about it and never treated me as a bad child because I wasn't. All I would say when confronted about the incident was, "I didn't do it." I was shown the awful marks on the girl's body. She had large areas of broken skin, scratches, and scarring. It looked terrible. Her hand looked as if it was burned on a hot stove. It was hard for me to feel empathy or sympathy because I honestly thought I didn't do anything.

One time when all the students were at gym class with the gym teacher, playing hockey, the girl was trying to be nice to me. She asked if she could be goalie with me. After that the only thing I remember is being back in the classroom once again. My teacher had to call her mom and my mom. She was left with marks on her body from what I was told again came from me. It's hard to believe you did something when you obviously don't remember. Her family moved and placed her in a new school at Newington. I was left asking my mother, "Did she move because of me?" My mom said that she didn't think so, but either way I felt bad. I felt remorse as if I was a bad child.

No one in school at that time treated me like I was a bad child, which made me feel better. I felt comfortable around my teacher and the women who watched me in the before and after school program. My mom was a single mom, and my dad wasn't present in my life so I would stay at the program until she got off work. This was a program I enjoyed. Before school started, we would get snacks, juice, and were able to do activities. After school we would go outside, do arts and crafts, play card games, and get our nails painted.

Being here before and after school sparked my creative side with arts and crafts. When my mom would come and get me after school I would ask her to go to an arts and crafts store so I could get string. She would always take me, and I would come home and make string bracelets. I briefly started a string business when I was seven years old and sold some jewelry to one of my family members.

My mom had always encouraged me to do whatever I loved, and she was also protective of me. She didn't like anyone treating me unfairly and took action towards anyone who did. I'll never forget when I was six years old in the first grade. I had a teacher who was very stern, strict, and no nonsense. One time I was seated at my desk and my foot was out. She walked by and kicked it in.

I told my mom, and she was not happy. She called the school and told the principal. The principal said that he would talk to her, but he was weak and didn't do anything. Then she called my teacher while she was at work and asked her what happened. My teacher's response to my mom was, "I put her foot back in with my hand." My mom's reply to that was, "That's not what my daughter said, and I believe her." They went back and forth, my mom ended up yelling at her, and they both concluded that she was not to put her hands on me.

After this conversation it was smooth sailing in this class. Most of the time my hair was in cornrows. To this day I don't wear braids or cornrows in my hair because my mom would braid or cornrow my hair and add beads all the time. The school I went to was predominantly white, so the students had a different background and culture from me. I spent a lot of time around my family who grew up at North End of Hartford, Connecticut. Newington was a suburb and Hartford was the ghetto.

My mom grew up in one of the toughest neighborhoods in Hartford, called Bellevue Square. She enjoyed her childhood and was thankful for the way she was raised, but she also saw how bad it was. Due to the enormous crime rates, and countless crimes she witnessed she moved to Newington to give me a better life.

I remember there was one girl in my class who took more to melanated people than white. I taught her how to do the butterfly dance. It was all the rage in the nineties for melanated people. My mom had taught me this dance. It was nice to be around some people who did embrace me, but it certainly wasn't easy. I was heavily misunderstood and was constantly calling people racist for excluding me.

Whenever I was around my family at Hartford, I felt loved and wanted to go to school with family members in my age bracket. It was a culture shock to be around them and then go to school around a bunch of stuck up, racist students. Most of the students at my school came from upper middle class to rich families and had two parents. I came from a broken home and was considered middle class.

It was hard to get in touch with my father and he rarely came to see me. When my mom and I would call, his wife would pick up the phone and lie for him. He wouldn't talk to me and made promises to come get me, but never did. I didn't know what depression was back then but looking back I had depression.

My father left me with feelings of uncertainty, anxiety, and rejection. I wasn't accepted in school and felt as though my father didn't accept me either. To add fuel to the fire, my father married a white woman, adopted her children, and took care of them as his own. I could not care less if she was white or not. It's the fact he abandoned me for her and her family that I had an issue with.

The times he would come and get me were on my birthday and I felt nervous and depressed. As a child I knew how I felt but didn't delve deeply into why I felt that way. Now I know that the nervousness and depression I felt was due to the fact that I was around my father temporarily. I wasn't sure if I was going to see him again, and I felt as if he wasn't my father but more their father. Here came the feeling of rejection once again. I remember Saturdays waiting on him to come pick me up. I would sit in my room and watch the music videos on the television. Artists, such as Jewel, Paula Cole, Spice Girls, and more would come on. The song that stood out to me, capturing my hurt and sadness was, *Where Have All The Cowboys Gone?* by Paula Cole.

This song evoked so much emotion in me and also relaxed my depression. At that time this song was the best friend who understood me. It was my comfort. Although my father didn't come to pick me up most of the time listening to those songs made me feel better. When he did come to pick me up his car smelled of alcohol and cigarettes. I used to love this smell because that's how he smelled all of the time.

He is the reason why I love oldies music. The Four Tops was one of his favorite groups. *Same Old Song* became a favorite song that I loved to listen to. Although his car smelled like alcohol and cigarettes he was never drunk when he came to pick me up. However, he was an alcoholic who dabbled in drugs and was a chain smoker. I remember telling my mom when I was five years old that I saw my dad dying due to smoking cigarettes.

She listened, but my mom was not a spiritual person. She didn't take it seriously. The inconsistent behavior displayed by my father and the recurring death dreams I kept having made me feel as though he was going to be a temporary person in my life. I could never feel settled or at peace around him. He could have done better as a father. He did buy me a ring and clothes for my birthday, but he wasn't present throughout the week.

When I was eight years old, one Christmas he came to my house. He usually had a mustache, beard, and eyebrows. I looked at him and said, "Where are your eyebrows? What happened to your eyebrows? Did you get them cut?" I was shocked to see him like this. There was no forewarning. My father had a tendency to pop in and out of my life and be sporadic most of the time. He sat down and told me he had lung cancer. He had lost his eyebrows due to chemotherapy. When he told me this, I felt like I was losing him and my excitement for the day dissipated. I was instantly sad and not looking forward to going over to his house. Christmas intensified those emotions because it was a day that family came together, and I felt like my family was disappearing.

I also asked him if he was going to die, and he said he wasn't. He was being protective of me and told me something that would bring me comfort. This was the one time that he should have lied to me I guess, but other times he lied for no reason. My father struggled to tell the truth.

The only time I recall him answering with a yes or no response was when I asked him about the eyebrows and when I asked if he would shoot 'Monster', the piece of shit who abused me with a gun. His response to that question was, "Yes". My father was not the emotional type at all. I never saw him cry. He was firm and stoic. Even when he told me he had cancer he didn't seem sad. I was sad when I found out, but I made sure not to cry in front of him.

That day he drove me to his house where he lived with his wife and her three children he adopted. She had two boys and one girl. They always treated me well as if I was their little sister. His wife looked older than her age. Her children's biological father was a pedophile. Although they were usually pleasant to me one of the siblings acted a bit different towards me that day. The day when I needed love the most, she was giving me an attitude for no reason. It was an awful day.

I had to watch my father's wife feed him food she made because he was too weak to do it himself. I didn't enjoy any of my food. I could feel the tears well up internally as I was sitting at the table eating that bland cabbage she made. It took everything out of me not to cry. I was glad when his wife brought me home because I was able to release all those emotions. This was an extremely emotive time for me. Slow songs started to make me cry because they reminded me of him and his being sick. Yet, I had faith that he would get better because he was still alive for months later.

The day that I looked forward to during this difficult time in my life was Field Day. I was in third grade in another one of my favorite teacher's classes. She taught us to treat each other with respect. She didn't see different complexions and she loved all of us equally. When I wasn't in my teacher's class I was learning about respect in Brownies. I was a part of the Girls Scouts organization and would participate in the extracurricular activities that came with that. I loved earning badges. My mom would sew them on, and I remember how happy I was. I smiled every time I received a new badge. One of my favorite field trips was to some place where they re-enacted the 1800s. They made us flapjacks and I remember wanting more than one. I was always hungry with undiagnosed diabetes. I was the child who ate all the pretzels and was shaky. I was also always thirsty.

It was fun attending the Memorial Day Parade. I felt special and as if all eyes were on me as I walked with my Girl Scout troop. There was only one other girl who was melanated in my troop. Her mom always wanted to fit in with other people, which got on my nerves. My teacher that year was down to earth and embraced everyone.

I loved when she taught on rights for melanated people and brought awareness to how we were targeted as a people. It made me feel understood. It was important to her to build a safe community in her classroom. As the year was winding down, we all participated in Field Day. I remember wearing a red hat, playing sports, having fun, and finishing out the day with a popsicle. When Field Day was finished, we all went back to the classroom.

It was a great day and a welcome relief from the sadness I was experiencing, but suddenly a teacher walked up to me and told me that my mom was here. I walked out in the hallway and saw my mom wearing sunglasses. Instantly I knew something was wrong. She was crying and said, "Your father died."

Immediately I burst into tears. As we were walking to her car. I said, "What happened to a second chance?" I was in disbelief and all these emotions circled me all at once. I wanted to see my father, hug my father, but felt distant from him. He died on June 4, 1998, of lung cancer.

A few months before dying, he was in hospice. My mom, aunts, and I went to visit him after Church. I was so nervous to see him in hospice. He hugged me and was strong. His eyebrows grew back and because of this I thought he was getting better. Unfortunately, he didn't make it. I took time off from school and with my family members, attended his funeral on June 8, 1998.

I remember walking up to my father's casket and seeing him with glue on his eyes. The funeral home did a horrible, fucking job. They gave him too much embalming fluid and he was unrecognizable. It was a sad day. I cried especially when my father's wife's sister sang. My father's adopted daughter from his new marriage was crying and saying, "I want my dad." This made me mad because I was his real daughter. Everything started to hit me when she was saying that. I was thinking about how I really didn't get to spend time with him, and she did.

I was thinking about how he spent more time with his wife and new family. I felt betrayed, alone, and instantly disconnected from him. It was as if I didn't belong and to top it off, I was excluded from riding with his wife's family in the limo. I asked her if I could ride with them and she said, "I'll have to ask...We'll see." She never gave a response.

What a bitch?! I started to see she was a fake person. When the people in charge of the burial asked her if she wanted his jewelry or wanted him buried with it, she declined the jewelry. I wanted to speak up so badly but couldn't find the strength to do so. I regretted not asking for his jewelry because I wanted to keep it.

My paternal grandmother was also at the funeral acting like the dramatic, heartless piece of shit she was. Her pedophile husband, 'Monster' did not attend the funeral because he wasn't allowed around me and my father had no dealings with him because of what he did to me. She treated her son like shit. My father was never good enough for her.

She loved his brother more than she loved him, but fake cried and made a dramatic scene at the funeral. I didn't want to hug my paternal grandmother after the funeral, but a family member asked if I wanted to hug her, but I felt reluctant. I walked up to her, and she looked as though she didn't want to hug me. She didn't say hello. didn't ask how I was doing, nothing. I instantly regretted hugging her and thankfully out of my thirty-two years of life, that was my only interaction I had with her since the abuse I suffered in her demonic ass apartment.

My father was a Marine, so he was buried along with the Veterans. After his burial a family member drove me to Burger King, and I got a Whopper. I couldn't really enjoy my Whopper that much and on such a sad day and she had a horrible attitude to this. I don't recall what she said, but I recall how she made me feel and it wasn't pleasant. About a week later my father's wife had a phone call with my mom and me.

She talked about going out to eat at Friendly's, but it never happened. I never heard from her or saw her again. She has never tried to make contact with me.

However, I appreciated my teacher who was so thoughtful during this rough time of my life. She had everyone in my class send me encouraging letters and letters of condolences. They made a big postcard for me. It was huge! This made me feel better and as if people did care about me. She had empathy and an intuition that was unmatched. She was a caring person who I needed at that time. It took a while to get over my father's death.

Although his death was hard, I felt relieved, and I stopped feeling depressed. The feeling of always waiting for him to show up and wondering why he spent time with people who were not related to him went away. Sure, I still felt rejection and had to heal from that, but the sadness and emptiness were gone. I know this may sound bad, but this is how I felt.

I came to terms with the fact that my peace was important, and it was okay to feel that way. The only sadness I felt was from mourning his death. Another family member of mine told me to think that my father was on vacation. This helped me for a while, but it hit me when I realized he was never coming back. I was out of school for a bit so I could grieve properly.

When I came back to school I would cry out of nowhere. I'll never forget crying during lunch in the cafeteria. I was so pitiful as I was eating my chicken nuggets. I was chewing and crying, feeling the saliva and the tears. It was a horrible experience that I would never want again. Some of the students were cold towards me and not pleasant while I was crying.

I had a great, supportive mom and family that helped me at that time. People who I was extremely close to were helpful. A family member always took my cousins and I everywhere. We went to the pool, restaurants, amusement parks, and various other places. She was instrumental in making my life joyous. I always had something fun to look forward to.

Summers were my favorite because I went swimming all the time and attended a summer program. I was like a little mermaid. I would get lost in the water. When I was eight I took swimming lessons and almost passed, but the swimming instructor took one point off for a move that I thought I did correctly. I was pissed because I had worked so hard and thought I did well. I liked to excel and was competitive. When I heard I didn't pass I felt like I was staying back in school.

I didn't take the swimming test again and instead swam in the deep end and all the levels of the pool anyways. Her approval wasn't needed, and I moved on with my life, but boy did I give her an attitude when she told me I didn't pass. I had a permanent frown on my face for more than an hour. I went to this program for most of the Summer and then a family member watched me the rest of the time until I went back to school.

I spent my summer on the North End of Hartford. I looked forward to going there each year because there you had to grow up fast. My cousins and I would take the bus downtown and go to the stores by ourselves. It was a dangerous area, but we had so much fun and great memories. My family member made us breakfast, lunch, and sometimes dinner if I didn't go home early. There were times when she was strict, and it made me uncomfortable. I was a bit hesitant to say things to her. For example, when I cut my foot on wood outside and bled everywhere, I thought I was going to get in trouble.

However, I loved being over there and we had so much fun. She would take us to get our nails done and we would go out to eat at various restaurants. She wasn't the affectionate type but showed how she felt with actions. Having fun meant everything because as a child I would hide the dark forces I battled daily.

I felt like an angel around my family member who took us to amusement parks and various places, my mom, other family members, but weird and disgusting when I was home. The sexual abuse and physical abuse I suffered at the hands of Monster made me feel as though I was different from everyone else.

I felt guilty because what happened to me was so dark. I felt alone, as if I needed to be rescued, and as if no one could help me. I was confronted with many different spirits I had to fight against, and they were wicked and dark. Everything from depression to rage was a constant battle. When you go through abuse it opens a world of darkness. What you knew to be innocent in life was no longer innocent.

I knew there were criminal minds out there and I was violated by one of them. I felt angry and regretful for many years after this traumatic experience. As a child I didn't know how to heal myself fast enough to feel whole again. It was as if I was existing in this world, but not living. I felt like an outcast and distant from everyone else. I felt distant from my mom because she was so innocent and peaceful. She hadn't gone through what I went through. I wish that had never happened to me and I didn't understand why it did for a long time.

I am forever thankful to one of my family members for providing an outlet for me to have fun and be around my cousins who helped me forget about my issues. They saw me as their cousin, and she saw me as her niece. I wasn't an outcast or disgusting to them.

Although when she had sleepovers, I was not the crowd favorite amongst them and was an outcast, we loved each other and were very close. I don't remember what I used to say, but it was irritating to them, I guess. They said hurtful things to me as well and we simply didn't get along during the sleepovers. I can recall my family member that was watching us telling me that I had to find my niche.

She knew I didn't fit in. I hated the sleepovers. I only had one cousin that I got along with during those sleepovers, but still wanted to go home each time. I felt trapped and depressed. I despised feeling trapped and people being mean because that is what I experienced in my early years. I'm sure I played a part in this as well and said provoking things. Thankfully we stopped having sleepovers because I was not going to attend ever again.

Although we had out bad moments our love never changed for each other. They were the first real friends I knew growing up. The sleepovers were not an outlet for me, but going places were and so was playing an instrument.

CHAPTER 2

When I was nine years old, I was given the opportunity at my school to play an instrument. This was a great day for me because I was going to learn something new. At first, I picked up the flute and my mom didn't want me to play flute because of the mouthpiece. She thought they shared mouthpieces and they did so she was grossed out.

The next day I went back to school and chose a different instrument. I decided to pick up the violin. The middle school students came over to the elementary school to show us how to play the instrument. I immediately knew that I was meant to play violin because when I picked it up and started playing there were no scratching noises. Typically, when anyone starts to play violin it will sound like scratching and hitting different strings.

When I played there was a clear sound and I didn't hit the other strings. I still remember how my bow glided across the D string and that rich noise that projected from it. It was absolutely perfect coming from a nine-year-old, inexperienced child. My mom was thrilled when I told her that I wanted to play violin and she took it very seriously. In the summer I started violin lessons with a woman at a local music center.

She was a highly eccentric and free-spirited cat lady who played violin. She had a classical background. The Suzuki method was something she taught me, but she didn't teach it properly. I had fun with her and enjoyed my lessons, but as I got older, I realized there were many holes in her teaching strategies. The fundamental basics were not taught. Instead, she taught me how to play songs and vibrato. I felt as if I was moving quickly and was talented. I played well, but wasn't taught how to hold the violin correctly, the bow correctly, and various bowing techniques were skipped over. She taught me for about a year and was fired from the music store. I was ten during this time and that same year I had a concert at a middle school in Newington, Connecticut. This was such an exciting time for me because it was my performance debut.

I played *Allegro* from one of the Suzuki books and I nailed it. I wasn't nervous one bit and was more concerned about showcasing my talent than anything. When people clapped for me, I felt exuberantly overjoyed. It was the greatest sense of accomplishment.

After my performance my orchestra teacher asked me if I would like to go and teach the elementary students. It was an honor to be asked to teach the elementary students and I agreed with no hesitation. Along with playing violin I enjoyed singing and acting. I can recall one day finishing my lunch and going to audition for the talent show.

I sang *Hero* by Mariah Carey. Five girls were picked, and I was not one of them. Shortly after I was asked to be in the talent show because one of the girls was unable to make it. I was so happy, but unfortunately couldn't attend. My mom was a Christian Sunday School teacher and not supportive of singing that kind of music. She had gotten saved when I was seven and after that it was all gospel music.

She didn't know how important this was to me. I was very sad and felt like I was missing out. I didn't let her know that this bothered me until years later. My mom, a family member, and I went to the mall that day instead. This was devastating, but another opportunity came along, and this was huge for a ten-year-old. I had the chance to audition for the play *Evita* and I poured my heart and soul into it. I was picked to sing in the play and this time my mom let me do it. The songs weren't seen as bad, so she was supportive. This was a big production that was put on by the high school in Newington.

I missed days of school to participate in this musical and it was a great experience. Each day I was able to eat pizza and talk with my friends. Other students had auditioned to be in the children's choir like I did. I got to meet new people but wasn't one to talk to anyone I knew was phony. I spotted a couple people that talked about other people, and I steered clear of them. I felt peaceful that way.

Missing school for ten days, eating pizza, and singing felt like a dream and a continuous field trip. I enjoyed watching the musical in the audience and backstage. We rehearsed for ten days and performed for three days. It took an enormous amount of work to put this production together, but it was all worth it in the end. This was one of the best times of my life.

I was no stranger to the arts. My mom was a talented play-wright, and she conducted the church choir for many years. I've been singing and doing plays since I was five years old. My cousins and I were talented. We did plays, we sang, and went to various churches to do so. Theater was fun because I was able to be different characters.

My mom specialized in bringing characters to life by giving them their own unique personalities. I enjoyed doing elderly characters the most. It brought joy to make other people laugh, while expressing life lessons through acting. I knew I wanted to sing when I saw Whitney Houston singing, *I'm Every Woman*. I would sing her song with my Nickelodeon microphone from McDonald's. I sang solos in church and sang along with my cousins. However, many people at the church, some family included, were not encouraging. I felt talented and as if I shined when I was at school. My mom, the pastor, and some family members were appreciative of my talents, but other adults didn't really say anything. I was the child who isolated themselves from bad vibes and put my energy towards people who appreciated it. I was always the talented one at school and wasn't celebrated at church or by many family members.

I could count on my hand the people in the family who said kind things to me. I was called beautiful or smart by a small amount of people. Back then I didn't know about love language, but compliments are a love language to me. I was also not a crowd favorite. I remember someone that was close to the family would take all my cousins, and not me, places.

I recall a close family friend that went to the church who bought my cousins things and took them on trips but left me behind. I felt as though adults didn't like me but loved my cousins. Even on holidays adults would get some of my cousins gifts and leave some of us out. My mom and some other family members thought about me each time. I adored my cousins but felt like the adults brought about a separation.

As a child I thought adults were trying to create a divide between my cousins and me. However, as I got older, I realized they weren't doing this intentionally. As someone who had experienced severe trauma and rejection countless times, I promised myself that I wouldn't let that get to me. The rejection that I felt only fueled my passion for my creative endeavors. I pursued a career in music.

When I was eleven years old a new violin teacher came into the local music store. She smelled like musty milk. She was stricter and better than the last one, but I was bored with her. She taught me more than the last teacher but ignored some of the basics. Sometimes I thought she was bribing me to stay there by giving me chocolate. She was thoughtful and I stayed with this teacher from age eleven to sixteen and then moved onto a teacher who had her own studio.

I started violin auditions when I was eleven. I'll never forget the early Saturday auditions. I was a late sleeper so getting up that early was not the norm for me. However, I was dedicated. On my first audition I scored a 72 out of 85. Auditions were off to a great start.

This was the beginning of a series of auditions. During this time, I was in the 6th grade with a teacher who I didn't like initially. She wasn't my favorite teacher at first because I didn't understand her. She was strict and wasn't the affectionate type, so I didn't know where to place her. I had problems with some of the students in the class. This one boy used to pick on me and I would hit him. Another time I shoved a girl and she dropped to the floor. I didn't feel bad hitting people. As a matter of fact, I craved hurting other people who crossed me. When the students said something to me that I didn't like I hurt them with physical force. I was never one for talking. For example, when I was in third grade class there was a girl who said or did something I didn't like. I waited days until all of us were in gym class to get her back. That day we played hockey and I had a stick. I saw her coming and I hit her in the face, blunt force with the hockey stick. I made it look like an accident and asked her, "Are you okay?" Inside I was happy as all hell. Her face immediately turned black and blue.

She was badly bruised, and I didn't care. I went home, ate my snacks, and watched my favorite television shows. There was another incident back at the summer program where this girl hit me. I hit her back, then she hit me again, and this continued until I got tired. I took her entire body, swung her, and then dropped her on the cement floor. After that I blacked out and the only way, I knew I blacked out was when I saw her at the program a different day. I said, "What happened to your arm?"

Her arm had huge brown/red scratches on it. She replied, "You did it." How she got scratched was beyond me.

My 6th grade teacher saw these violent behavioral patterns within me. She observed me until one day she put me in Anger Management. The last incident I remember before I went to Anger Management was when I stabbed another boy with a pencil. The boy was picking at me while I was doing my work so I stabbed him with my pencil so he would stop. He stopped and said, "Ow". I went back and finished my work like I hadn't done anything.

Anger Management was not a place I wanted to go but I was ordered to attend during lunch. This took me away from the cafeteria and my classmates and I thought it was boring. My teacher told my mom that I was in Anger Management and at first my mom didn't understand why. Once told the reason why, she agreed to keep me in there. It was boring and I didn't like it, but it taught me a lot. I started to calm down and use my words to convey what I felt inside rather than my fists. I stopped hitting people and talked to them instead. I was tested after I left Anger Management though. Someone got mad at me, and I stood my ground, but I didn't hit her. The old me would have punched her in the face with no hesitation and she would have been badly injured.

I'm thankful to that teacher until this day because at the rate I was going I would have been in jail. She became one of my favorite teachers and she was happy that I transformed. She used to talk about how she loved the play *Aida* and thought I looked like the beautiful melanated princess. She always encouraged my self-esteem in her own way.

. . .

That was a great school year filled with lessons and I missed her when I entered 7th grade. When I was 12 going to school was very different. The students were no longer friends with everyone. They had divided into groups and there were now nerdy people, popular people, skaters, and more. I was always away for the summer so when I came back, I had no clue where I fit in.

I had a fun summer that year although it started off a little scary and shaky. I found out my mom was taken to the hospital on an emergency; she had to have a hysterectomy due to endometriosis. I thought she was going to die. This was the paranoia I suffered from after my father died early in life. Thankfully she didn't, but she was admitted to the hospital. I had to stay over my maternal grandmother's house for a week. My other family members stayed there as well. We had fun and went to the library. I studied a lot of history on melanated people and watched music videos. *Carmen The Hip Hopera* had just come out and it was something I looked forward to watching.

My mom finally came home, and life was even more fun. We laughed, watched television, and a family member came to take my cousin and I to the library. My maternal grandmother made the best food so that was another fond memory I had of that experience.

For part of that summer, I attended Music Camp where the high school orchestra teacher was teaching me and other teachers I didn't like so much. The teacher had favorites in the orchestra. I was not the favorite and always felt as if I had to compete, but I played very well. We had to learn music theory amongst other things. The teachers made it so boring and didn't teach it to where I could understand it. It made me feel as though I was behind, but I was determined not to give up on the violin. It was a tough instrument, but I made it through to the end of the program.

The students and I came from different schools, but we got to know each other. It was a bit rough at first, but things improved. The performance ended up being amazing. The night of the performance my mom taught Bible Studies. She turned it into a field trip and brought my cousins and the people in the Bible Studies class with her to watch that performance.

That same year I was going through a bit of depression being in that program. Looking back, I really didn't want to be around people who were so different from me and didn't understand me. I got fucking tired of being the underdog and always having to prove myself. I remember when Kelly Osbourne came out with a single, *Papa Don't Preach*. When I watched that I felt a sense of acceptance.

She dressed differently and had an emo, goth, punk rock, and retro look. I thought about cutting my hair the way she had it styled in the video. I even tried to wear a belt and heels after I watched it. I felt like I fit in and was understood. She was popular but had her own unique look. This uplifted my spirits when I felt depressed and alone.

Shortly after this, when I went back to school, I saw that I didn't fit in at all and on top of that my hormones were out of whack. I started my period when I was ten years old and started to develop PMS when I was twelve. This was a horrible combination. I went from being carefree and uninhibited to being a nervous wreck. I was shaky when I had to read and present in class in front of other people.

I recall this pale girl asking me a question and as I was answering she rudely cut me off and said, "Whatever". It was strange going from the girl who spoke to everyone just a year ago to a shy, nervous girl who wanted to stay home from school. I used to practically beg people to sit with me at lunch. It was weird because in Hartford, I was loved and welcomed by my cousins and some family, but at school I was a nerd and an outcast.

I would sometimes grab my lunch and beg my orchestra teacher to let me sit in there with her. That way I didn't have to sit by myself. Eventually she got tired of me sitting in there with her. I remember a new girl who was a couple years older than everyone came to my school She had stayed back for whatever reason. She was sitting with another girl, and they were the cool girls. I saw an open seat and sat there. They looked at me weirdly, but didn't say anything. I nervously sat there and ate my cheeseburger. At this point in my life, I was self-conscious about everything - my breasts were huge, I wore glasses, and I was chubby. In addition, my bra didn't fit me properly and wasn't flattering. Everyone was wearing the latest outfits and I was still wearing Winnie the Pooh. My glasses were still thick, and I still had a strong prescription. I hated the small pair of square glasses with black rims I had to wear in 7th grade. I also had a roller backpack and most of my clothes were from Old Navy, Wal-Mart, or from a cousin. I used to beg my mom to bring me to the store where the other children bought their clothes. Many of the children wore Weathervane or Gap. I got one hoodie from Weathervane and was overjoyed. I still didn't fit in, but I did talk to a couple girls. I sat with one of them at lunch and while doing so, one of the so-called popular girls came over and said, "Why are you sitting with her?" The girl I was sitting with didn't want to make me feel bad or anything and she expressed to me how mean those girls were.

Although most of the year was horrible for me, I was excited that this was the year all the 7th graders got to take a trip to Williamsburg. At first, I was homesick, but soon began to have fun. It was an incredible experience because besides New York I had never gone to any other place. I loved eating breakfast at Best Western Hotel and enjoyed feeling independent. Although there was adult supervision, they let us wander off. I got to bond with some of the girls there and everyone was more welcoming. The Salem Witch Trial re-enactment was my favorite experience there. It was realistic and I felt as though I could relate to it.

When the week was over, I didn't want to return home. That was a trip I'll never forget. This was the year for trips. One of my family members used to put New York shopping trips together for all the church members. I loved traveling and going to new places. The people in New York were hustlers and very welcoming. The best part was listening to my music when traveling there and listening to it when I got back. I'm still this way. I could have an incredible, life-changing experience in a different location, but there's something about traveling while listening to music that makes everything better. New York became my second home. I loved it there. Every street looked different, no one dressed the same, and it made me feel like I fit in somewhere. Everyone had unique styles and talents in the Big Apple. It was a great vibe. There were a variety of vendors and food places, and it wasn't a boring place. I went to New York every year and it was always an enjoyable experience. The school year ended on a positive note and the summer was fun.

One of my family members took my cousins and I to Six Flags again. That was the year that Styles P came out with *Good Times* and Toshamakia came out with *Be Yourself*. He loved to play music excessively loudly which I loved. It was a fun ride back and forth. Rollercoasters and amusement parks warmed my heart and gave me the thrill I was looking for. Euphoria was what I felt. My Aunt had been taking my cousins to Six Flags since I was five years old. It used to be called Riverside Park back then. As a child I hated riding the little children's rides. My cousin and I had to ride the children's rides because we were one year apart in age. I looked forward to when I got older and could get on more thrill-seeking rides. My Aunt was also a rollercoaster lover. Our favorite rollercoaster was, The Flashback. This was a ride that went backwards. I always had to give my glasses to the conductor. One time we were on this rollercoaster and I for sure thought I wasn't strapped in. I was afraid that I was going to fall out of the seat.

I told my aunt and tried to tell the person who conducted the ride that I was going to fall out, but everyone was screaming with excitement. Thankfully I was fine, but I was scared. Whenever I was hesitant about trying a new ride, my older cousin would go on the ride with me and/or encourage me to get on.

The fried dough, ice cream, the fries, and the dipping dots were delicious at the time and elevated the excitement of being at the amusement parks. My aunt was a super special person in my life. Every day was a celebration with her, and she made my birthdays special. She would take us to Six Flags on my birthday. She took us everywhere. Life was truly an incredible adventure with her and my cousins. When the summer was over it was time to go back to school once again. There was no summer program when I was in middle school, so I spent the summer over my other aunt's house.

When I wasn't at my aunt's house my mom would spend time with me and take me out to eat and to the movies. This was a yearly tradition with my mom and I. I always looked forward to seeing the latest movies and eating. We would have fun cracking jokes and laughing.

As summer came to an end I was going into 8th grade. It was my last year of middle school and I was still unpopular. People were in cliques, and it was worse than the year before. Many of the students bonded and were suburban. I spent my days and nights at Hartford, on the North End; an area considered the ghetto it was more fun and freer.

I couldn't relate to the other students. Even people who were from Hartford that were bused to Newington didn't really accept me. They accepted the other students from Newington even though most of them who didn't look like them. I didn't feel I fit in anywhere. I was still sometimes sitting by myself at lunch or included myself at someone's lunch table. I felt like an unwanted guest. I'll never forget when I was emotional on my father's born day. The girls were mean and didn't want me at their table. I was thankful I had a family member who moved back to Newington and came to the school, but I still had nowhere to sit during lunch. Although I could have sat with him, I didn't want to intrude. He was one of the cool people and all the boys wanted to fit in with him. I felt better when he was there. More people started to respect me and got to know me. Some were being fake people, and some liked me as a person. I still felt alone at school and had developed an eating disorder at this time. I would make a sandwich and made a smiley face with the cheese cubes, tomatoes, and mayonnaise. I ate that every day and lost some weight.

I told my mom that I didn't want to attend school anymore and that I was depressed. Her advice to me was that it's best not to fit in and who cares if those people don't like me. She thought it was cool to be different. My mom wasn't able to homeschool me because she had to work so we could survive. Eventually one of the girls at school and I became friends. She let me sit at her table and she was kind to me.

The boys didn't ask me out like they did the other girls, but some were attracted to me. I had my second sexual encounter with a boy when I was thirteen. It was nothing serious, but he touched and rubbed my breasts and top half of my body. That was it. I was eight years old when I had my first sexual encounter. The boy and I were around the same age.

I would consider this an exploration phase we went through. We both got naked, and he licked and sucked my breasts. I started growing breasts at age six and was about a B cup at that time. Boys always flirted with me at Hartford and New York, but they weren't as open at Newington. I had a huge crush on this one boy. It was the same boy who used to pick on me in 6th grade. He always smelled good and had a fresh haircut. I used to call him countless times on the phone until he answered. I never did this again, but I was young and dumb at the time. I remember when I arrived at school early one day. One of his friends was standing next to him. His friend turned to me and said, "He doesn't like you."

My response was, "Oh okay I don't care."

I kept moving and went about my day. This was an empowering moment for me because I didn't let the rejection get me down. His friend was so proud of me. The boy I had a crush on felt bad and didn't want to tell me himself. After that I didn't have any feelings for him.

We were all in the same class with this teacher from hell. She was a bitch, and I couldn't stand her. She never smiled and never had anything good to say to me. I was never good enough and to her, mediocre. She showed favoritism to one student. I remember when my mom had a parent/teacher conference with her. She kept calling me, The Kid. My mom hated it and told her to stop calling me that. She was putting me down and my mom wasn't standing for it. She let her have it. My grades were not the best in her class, and I couldn't wait to graduate so I could leave.

Going to High Meadow was the only fun I had to look forward to that year. Everyone went to High Meadow before the year's end. There was a bouncy house, games, the pool, food, and music. I bought a pair of jeans that I couldn't fit at the beginning of the year, but since I wasn't eating that much, I was able to fit them.

They were tight-fitted and not my normal attire, but I wore them to High Meadow. They showed my ass and that was my aim. I wanted to fit in with the other girls who were wearing tight clothes. I had fun dancing with my friend. We danced to Salsa music because I was a natural at that.

The same friend who was happy that I didn't care that the boy didn't like me, came up behind me and started grinding or dirty dancing. I was shocked because no one besides the other boy showed me any interest. This boosted my confidence. Overall, that was a fun experience, and the food was amazing. At graduation the friend that I was close to started acting funny and mean. This led to she and I going our separate ways. There was also drama over the summer with a situation that was blown out of all proportion.

That summer, as I was preparing for high school. I wanted to start fresh and change my appearance. I asked my mom if I could get contacts and she said I could. I was happy that I finally got to see how my natural face looked like without glasses. It was a dream come true to wear contacts. I didn't think I looked amazing, but I enjoyed looking at my face. I spent that summer around my cousins and my aunt again. We went to Six Flags almost every single day and never got tired. That was the summer Lumidee's, *Never Leave You* came out. My aunt went to church, so she didn't listen to that kind of music, but I asked her to play that song in the car as she drove us to Six Flags and turn it up. She did.

We were jamming in the backseat. I was glad to go to Six Flags without glasses because it felt less restrictive. I didn't have to worry about dropping them or losing them. Being around her and the people that loved me boosted my confidence. I no longer cared about fitting in with those other people. Being at Hartford I was more exposed to the real world and real life.

Students in my school were trying to be like the people out in the street. My family was from there and some were in the streets, well connected so that was nothing new to me. Towards the end of the school year, I had to go to the high school at Newington for orientation. My mom and I attended, and I was excited. I was confident and didn't give a flying fuck if I saw those girls that I didn't like. In fact, I wanted to see them. Some of them I did see, and they looked at me. I don't think they recognized who I was. Starting at a new school, with new people, and a clean slate filled my soul with excitement; I wanted to completely reinvent myself.

Back-to-school shopping was invigorating because I was determined to not wear anything from Wal-Mart. I also didn't want to fit in with the popular crowd anymore. I wanted to be my own person and create my own identity. I bought a variety of different outfits for the fall and wintertime, so I was prepared ahead. I wore a lot of headbands to school and loved sweat suits. I wore tight-fitted jeans, loose fitted jeans, and a variety of different outfits. I started to develop my individual style, one no one else, had. It made me feel like a leader and, at last, comfortable in my own skin.

My neighbor's mom used to bring her best friend and I to school. I'll never forget the first day ride to school because we listened to *Drop It Like It's Hot*. I loved that song. The neighbor introduced me to everyone at school. She fit in with different groups of people and I always had someone to sit with during lunch. She and I didn't get along all the time, and it was an off and on relationship. Eventually we stopped being friends and I was happy about that. She was the one who told me that someone from another school was going around telling everyone he had a crush on me.

I didn't know who he was, but it was flattering because people were chasing after me unlike in middle school. I found out that he was well known at the school he attended, and I eventually met up with him at the football game. He was very sweet, protective, and possessive. At the football game he had all eyes on me and we held hands. This was unusual because we came from different backgrounds. He was so called white and considered what most people call Puerto Rican as well. He wasn't my usual type, but he took the time to get to know me, paid me attention, and showed that he cared. I also liked his voice and he had swag. We never dated each other exclusively, but he always had a crush. When he found out I was attracted to someone else and was meeting with that person, he showed up at the house. He was jealous, but not in an evil way. That person cared about me, but I was attracted to an emotionally unavailable person because that's what my father showed me was real. This fear of real love made me mess up my first relationship in freshman year of high school.

My first boyfriend was the sweetest. We took absolutely no time to get to know each other. He was sixteen years old, and I was fourteen years old. Before he asked me out, I'll never forget passing him in the hallway. We were eyeballing each other like crazy. He had a smooth walk, and I was feeling myself in my tan/beige terry cloth zip up hoodie and bottoms.

My ass looked like a big peach. I wore a headband and had brown hair with strawberry blonde streaks. It wasn't too long after we exchanged eye glances in the hallway that he asked me to be his girlfriend. I accepted his offer and was happy to have a boyfriend. I looked forward to going to Junior Prom with him as well. He was the best boyfriend I ever had. He would walk me to my classes and tell my teachers to treat me well. When girls walked by, he wouldn't stare at them, and all eyes were on me. We would set a date and meet with each other after school. As soon as he saw me walking up the hallway he came and hugged me close. Again, there were other girls around, but he only saw me. One friend who was a jealous, promiscuous girl, thought he and I moved too fast. She even called him on the phone, but he didn't give her the time of day. I'm glad to not be friends with her and I never will be again. She was absolutely disgusting, had no morals, and no remorse for her actions. He didn't give in to her advances like the other boys did. She went with so many boys at my school and other schools.

I loved that he had the utmost respect for me and dismissed her. However, I started to question the relationship and my feelings for him because I didn't know him that well. I regretted the day I broke up with him. That day he was being a gentleman and getting to know my cousin who I went to school with. All of us walked out of the cafeteria together and I was trying to get my boyfriend's attention while he was talking to my cousin. He wasn't responding because he didn't hear me and that was my lame excuse to break up with him. I told him, "You're cut," and I left him standing in the hallway with my cousin. I wasn't ready for him or the love he had to give. He really liked me but at the time I was unsure of the depth of my feelings for him. So, instead of getting to know him better I broke it off. I think my daddy issues got the better of me. Real love was foreign and so were kindness and compassion from a man. The next day I felt so bad and wrote my now ex-boyfriend a letter of apology. He read it but didn't accept it. I broke his heart with my foolish actions and never meant to hurt him. We didn't get back together and went on about our lives, but he'll always be a special person to me and a rare person who treated me like an Empress. Although this relationship had long term potential, we were together for less than a week.

I started to like this boy who was from the same place the

boy I met at the football game was from. I spoke to him on the phone every day and finally met up with him at a friend's house. I remember play fighting with him and him choking me. He was serious even though I was playing. This was already a red flag, but this is what I was attracted to. I remember him sitting on the dresser in my former friend's room and holding my waist. We didn't do anything else, and it never went further than that. I found out he was attracted to another girl who looked nothing like me and was considered white. This made me upset, and I felt betrayed. When I went to lunch that day I was fuming. Some boy dared me to slap him for some odd reason; I was already mad, so I did slap him - so hard his face turned red.

He got upset and started coming towards me to hit me. My former friend stepped in and told him, "She's a girl." He backed off, but I got suspended from school for one day. Everyone heard about it, and I thought I was so cool for slapping the shit out of somebody.

For the most part I stayed out of trouble that year. I did well in school and loved my teachers. English was my favorite class, one in which I did very well. I remember not studying for a midterm and getting an 82 as a test score. I had a natural knack for reading and writing. It made me feel peaceful. There were some classes that I wanted to stay after school for and needed extra help in. Each time the teacher would stay after school I would blow them off to hang with my friends. I excelled in school, but my mind was on being social. For some reason none of my teachers would say anything to me the next day about not coming to get help after school.

One of the other classes I enjoyed was orchestra with one of my favorite teachers. He always joked and made orchestra fun. I remember him taking us to Central Connecticut State University on a field trip. We watched the Chamber Orchestra play and ate at the food court. I got the veggie burger and French fries. It was so good.

. . .

I was a fourteen -year-old vegetarian or so I thought. When I was twelve years old, I became a vegetarian, but as I got older I realized that I was actually a pescatarian. Back then even if you ate fish, you were still considered a vegetarian. My mom was a vegetarian because she didn't like eating animals and I wanted to try it out. I thought it was something different and a healthier option.

The first day I started to change my diet was the day my family and I went to Six Flags. Normally when I went to Six Flags, I got chicken and French fries, turkey leg, and fried dough. That day I forgot that I was a vegetarian and ordered a turkey leg with barbecue sauce. I took one bite and remembered that I wasn't supposed to eat that anymore, so I immediately gave it to someone who gladly ate it. When I told my cousins I was vegetarian one of them got upset for some reason and discouraged it. I didn't care what anyone thought and had to do what was best for me. One thing my mom instilled in me was to have a mind of my own, something which got me involved in orchestra as well.

No one in my family played an instrument and neither did any of my friends. Admittedly, I was ashamed to carry my violin and violin case around out of fear someone would make fun of me. I would have my mom drop me off to school early so no one would see me. She didn't understand it because she loved the violin and loved being different, but I didn't want anyone to categorize me.

People knew that I was in orchestra, but I didn't want it to define me that year. My orchestra teacher had put me in the first violin section. I'll never forget him. Another teacher started to quiz us on certain scales, and I had no clue as to what these were as my teacher at the music store didn't teach me them. I made it up but, despite not knowing, still got to play in the first violin section because I was a talented player with natural ability.

I had another violin competition that year. As I signed up for it last minute I had no clue what the violin piece was that I was supposed to be playing and didn't prep for it in any way. Sometimes I look back and ask myself, "What were you thinking?" I never played the piece but showed up to audition to play in the regional orchestra. I was very competitive with myself and wanted to be the best. On a Saturday morning I got up early and rode on the bus with other people who were also auditioning.

When we arrived at the audition site I saw one of my orchestra friends practicing, so I asked her for the piece and she taught me what she could over the next few hours. I walked into the audition and played confidently. I scored a 56 and even though I failed, that wasn't bad for not being prepared and practicing right before I entered.

My orchestra teacher didn't tell me what the piece was and people who judged my performance were upset by that. I was mad I didn't get to go to the next level and play in the regional orchestra but looking back I actually did pretty well. The violin wasn't an easy instrument to play and no one in their right mind would have even attempted to play a violin piece right before the audition. I was a true daredevil.

Still, I played *Pomp and Circumstance*, along with my school's orchestra at the graduation and had an immense amount of fun. We all took the bus there because it took place at Central Connecticut State University. It was nighttime so we were silly and laughed most of the time. I enjoyed watching other people graduate because it made me look forward to graduating in just three years.

CHAPTER 3

had a fun summer being around my friends, going over to my aunt's house, and going places I had no business being. My aunt moved out of Hartford, and I spent a lot of the summer over at her new peaceful place. There was a park, a gym, and a basketball court over there. I loved going on the swings and being outside. I remember wearing a baby pink t-shirt, khaki pants, and pink flip-flops from Old Navy. My hair was reddish blonde. I used to sneak off and talk to an older guy. He was a close friend of mine, turned best friend a bit later. He was five years older than me, and we would talk almost every day. I felt guilty doing this because no one in my family would approve, but I had a big crush on him. He was a bad boy and a rebel, who would speak his mind about anything to anyone and everyone. It was a turn on and the fact that he was older and showing me attention made me feel better about myself.

Occasionally a couple friends and I would go to his house. The first time I went to his house I got contact high. When I came home my mom, and I were watching *Pootie Tang* and I was being very silly. She didn't know why, but we were both laughing together so she thought we were simply having fun. I had a good night's sleep but woke up with the munchies. I used to eat a bagel with cream cheese and chips whenever I had the munchies.

That was one of many times I got high off on drugs. The second time I went over to his house he wasn't smoking. His friends were always over there. This time there was one of his friends, two of my (now former) friends, he and I there. They were talking and watching television. I was lying in the bed with him talking. I was on my period that night, but if I wasn't I may have thought about having sex with him. I wanted to but couldn't at the time. I told him I was on my period, so he started playing with my vagina through my pants. I had a great time with him, and the next time wanted to have sex, but it never happened. Once he was finished touching me my friend told me that she was getting phone calls from all our moms. I told my mom I was over a friend's house. She called and I wasn't there, so then she suspected I was over at a boy's house. Although she didn't know for sure, she was livid.

I was a free spirit and a rebel who liked to do what they wanted and enjoyed myself, but that night took a turn for the worse. When I got home my mom beat me with a belt. She beat me so bad, and I remember I did not cry. I was exposed to people who were from the streets, and they were tough, so I had developed a tough exterior and crying wasn't seen as tough. Although it hurt to be hit multiple times with a belt I refused to cry. The belt she hit me with left a permanent scar for many years, an indent on my left leg. I couldn't go to sleep easily that night at all and had to take Motrin 800 mg to get to sleep. I was in so much pain and was so achy all over that I wasn't able to go anywhere for a while. I still did what I wanted to do but became cleverer with my lies while I was out with friends. The life I lived when I was hanging out, I kept secret from my mom.

. . .

In the summer I went to Six Flags again with my aunt and cousins. We had fun per usual and made sure to ride on all the rides. The Tomahawk was my favorite. It was a circular ride and had seats for everyone. There were two rows of seats, and the ride went in a circular motion. Each time the Tomahawk would circle up in a higher motion than the last. Each time the speed would greatly increase as well. The best part about Six Flags was that there was a new ride most of the time and the old rides never lost their thrill and excitement. Most of us loved to ride so it brought more joy to ride with the ones you loved.

Those are memories I'll never forget. When the summer was over, and it was sophomore year I was fifteen years old. New freshmen were there, and it was a different vibe; not the same environment it was last year. The people were more authentic the previous year, but this year there was a lot of fakeness. I had also been friends with older people who graduated so they were gone, and I was stuck with younger people. I made new friends, but at this point I was tired of school. At the time I didn't know about being empathic or hypersensitive to energies, I just knew that I didn't like the environment. Going to New York, whether it was the Bronx, Harlem, or the Village to shop is what brought happiness into my life. I enjoyed going there because I felt free. There were no rules, nor groups of friends, and no drama. Hardly anyone I went to school with went to New York.

I used to frequent Dr. Jays in Harlem a lot to get the latest fashion. I never wanted to look like other people in high school. If people were wearing Timberland boots, I wore the Timberland red clogs. Many of the girls would get a French manicure and I would get marble nails with different colors. I had my hairdresser dye my hair blonde and I wore it curly. I shopped at many different places that none of the people I went to school with shopped. I wish I could have stayed in New York because at school I just felt depressed that year. School was un-enjoy-able. I used to ask my mom to home school me or send me to a Christian girl's school. One of the neighbor's daughters went to a Christian Academy and I asked my mom if I could go there. At the time my mom was a Christian Minister and would consult with the Holy Spirit or Holy Ghost to see if that was a good decision.

She definitely wasn't able to home school me as a single mom and didn't feel right about sending me to the Academy. I had to stay at the same school that I despised. One night after school let out there was a high school football game. There I met a guy from another school. He was huge in all aspects of the word. He took a liking to me and even told me that he was switching schools. Monday when I got back to school to my surprise he was there. He was eighteen years old and a senior. I was his main focus, but I started to see red flags. He would call me excessively to the point where I had to tell him to stop. We would get into arguments, and he would yell at me. Although we never had a title, and I was talking to different people, we kept trying to make it work. I remember seeing him in the hallway and him acknowledging me while talking to a friend. I had honey blonde, wavy and curly hair. I wore a long black shirt, some black dress pants, and suede boots with the fringes. My eyes had black smoky eye makeup on them. I thought I looked amazing. Leave it up to him to make me feel like shit. In front of his friend, he grabs my stomach and tells me that I need to work on that area. He had a big stomach but decided to tell me that I need to work on mine. After that I simply walked away from him and went about my day. I was tough, bold, and would speak my mind, but being around him, I started to feel abused. I felt owned and controlled. He was extremely possessive. I saw him in the hallway again and he kissed my cheek. I thought he was sweet right then and there, but I didn't like him as much as he liked me. My spirit was picking up on some red flags again. I would envision how it would be if he and I dated each other. I always feared us having sex and him not stopping when I said to stop or him making me do things against my will. His possessive side was overbearing and turned physically abusive. One day when I was walking in the hallway outside my English teacher's class he spotted me talking to another boy. I didn't like the boy I was merely being friendly.

The look on his face was one of sheer jealousy. He had a smirk and asked about the boy I was talking to. Then he close fist mushed my face. I said, "Ow," because it hurt. When I went on the bus to go home, I saw my face was swollen. I didn't tell anybody what happened, but I was thankful to my Spanish teacher who after the incident told us about a woman shot by her jealous boyfriend. He spoke to us and told us to be aware of all the signs. The signs he mentioned were - verbal abuse, hitting, constantly calling, stalking, and more. As I listened, I felt bad for the woman who was shot. She worked at my school and seemed very kind. I was also thinking about how the guy I was dealing with at the time did all of those things to me, and I instantly put a stop to it. After hearing that story, I found my inner strength to cuss him out, tell him to stop calling me, and then I completely ignored him and cut him off.

He stalked me and one day was at my bus stop. I walked right past him and didn't say a word. He eventually left the school I was at. I was cool with his friends and one of his friends informed me that the guy I cut off was saying he had sexual relations with me. We never got that far because I didn't feel safe with him. He started rumors and back then I simply thought he was abusive. I didn't know about narcissistic personality disorder or any of that. He was definitely a narcissist and a dangerous one at that. That was one of the problems I encountered that year. The boy's house I went over and got in trouble for was 20 at this time. We would talk on the phone on a weekly basis and sometimes multiple times a week. That same year he was arrested and placed in jail on misdemeanor charges.

At this time, I lost one of my best friends to prison and felt alone. I contacted one of his close friends and was able to locate him to write to him. Apparently, other girls were also writing to him. Although we weren't exclusive and there was no title I was pissed off. Months later he was released, and I found out. He didn't contact me, and I was mad at him. In a fit of pique, or perhaps retaliation, I decided to go and be with another guy I would never usually have given the time of day to. He wasn't my type in appearance or personality. He was considered, "Colombian". My friend had a crush on one of his friends, so we went to his house. He walked me up to his room and we started kissing. He lifted my shirt and rubbed my breasts. He tried to get me to give him oral sex and to have sex with him, but I declined. I was on my period once again and that wasn't in the cards that night. Usher, *My Boo* was playing in the background, but I wasn't with 'my boo'. I was with an idiot who had me locked in his room and constantly asked me for oral sex and sex. This went on for forty-five minutes, but I kept declining. Eventually I left his room, and we all went to the football game. When we arrived, I saw my best friend and we got into a small argument. We both accused each other of acting funny towards one another. That was the end of the conversation, and we didn't speak for a while. When I came back to school the next day people started acting differently towards me and treating me as if they didn't know me anymore. I found out the boy that tried to get me to give him oral sex but got denied, told everyone I did it. People started calling me a slut and different names. I had never been called a slut before. Most people believed the rumor that this idiot spread, and it went on for a long time. People I thought were my friends turned against me. Only one person stood up for me and we became friends. For most of the year I was miserable. I didn't really care for my teachers, the students, or the school. Between losing my best friend to prison and him paying other people attention, and the nasty rumors I contemplated suicide.

To add the icing on the cake I contracted the Herpes virus from kissing him. I remember my left eye kept itching and I was scratching it, but not getting relief. That itch turned into hurting and then into scabbing. The scab started to cover my eye and I told my mom. She took me to the doctor's office and he instantly told my mom that if she didn't get me to the eye doctor's office that I was going to go blind. I was placed on antibiotics and got the Herpes Virus in my eye every single year. It left me with astigmatism.

I could have thrown this entire year away in a dumpster and never looked back. As an outlet I used to cut myself frequently with kitchen knives, butcher knives, and razors. I never felt pain and people started noticing the scars on my arms. One person in Bible Study told me that it looked like Tic Tac Toe on my arms. I had scratch marks everywhere. One day when I was sitting in the bathtub, I wanted to end it all by slitting my wrists. I tried to cut my wrist with a razor, but I felt pain. Finally feeling actual pain made me discontinue my suicide attempt. I didn't bother to tell any of my family members who would have gladly whooped the boy's ass about the incident. I thought that was snitching so I kept it between my mom and me. I told my mom not to say anything. Some of my family members were well connected and well respected. They would have stepped in and scared the boy, but I never said anything.

As time went on, and as people got to know me, the rumors died down. That suicide attempt allowed me to refocus on the current beauty in my life. I became more ambitious and went after my goals. One of my goals was to get my permit and I accomplished that.

. . .

Another goal was to go to another school that had a focus on music. I wanted to switch schools and pursue a career in music, so I went to audition at this music school at Hartford. I played beautifully in front of a cellist who taught at Hartt Music School.

After I auditioned, I felt confident that I made it in. My future was looking brighter, and I started to feel accomplished. I walked around the school and into a jewelry making class. A woman was teaching the class how to make beautiful brass, copper, and silver bangles. Some people made rings and beaded bracelets as well. When I left the school, I felt as if I was on my way to pursuing a music career. I was happy to finally get the fundamental basics of learning the violin down.

However, it was not to be. The cellist was going to let me in the school, but her colleague was against it, and I had to audition again at his house. He was very nitpicky slighting the way I held the bow and even my violin. He wasn't willing to help me perfect this at the music school nor did he give me credit for the way I played the violin piece. After that audition I was denied entry to the school.

It was a disappointment, and I was fucking angry towards the man for denying me entry. I never gave up on my dream of being a professional violinist and even though I was rejected time and time again I still persevered. In the Spring I auditioned at a music collective on Albany Avenue at Hartford for a summer apprentice job. The focus of the collective was on dance and jazz. I remember wearing a long jean skirt and a colorful orange shirt to the audition. It's funny how some memories stay with you.

I was nervous to play in front of the man there, so I turned around and had my back to him. He accepted me into the program, and not only did I make it in, but I was also getting paid to play. This was a place that opened up opportunities for people from different backgrounds. There were music connections and people knew people associated with one of the top music schools in Connecticut.

I auditioned with Classical music, but it was a job where I had to play jazz. Prior to the job starting I went there to listen to a performance. I had on a jean jacket, some tight jean pants, and a colorful shirt. My hair was honey blonde and curly. There was an older man there. After the performance was finished and I was walking out to go home I could hear him speaking to the other melanated man I auditioned for. He yelled, "Culo" a Spanish word for 'butt' loudly. He thought I had a big ass. When the program started, and I had to play daily, he was there. He was one of the instructors. Playing in the style of jazz was no issue, however, improvisation wasn't my forte. I barely knew music theory and in order to do jazz improvisation you had to read certain chords, such as cMajor7, cDominant7, so forth and so on. That was like reading a foreign language to me.

No one there taught music theory and the way they were teaching others how to do improvisation wasn't helpful at all. One girl that played viola knew how to do improvisation, but I did not. One of the men there always said I had, fingertips and I had no clue what that meant. I was fifteen years old going on sixteen years old at the time and he was in his twenties. I discovered that fingertips meant that my breasts sat perky and they were perky enough for him to slide his fingers underneath.

He never got that chance and never said anything to me about wanting to take sexual action towards me. Him and I bumped heads. I even gave him the finger about a few things. He was moody. Another guy that worked there flirted with me a lot and I used to get so excited to see him every day. When it was my birthday, he gave me a lap dance. Despite the age difference I never felt they were being inappropriate because I felt as if I was older. In hindsight, I realize their behavior was inappropriate.

The man who I had recently met, and who I thought was my best friend, was also inappropriate. I was underage and there were things that shouldn't have gone on. However, I had feelings and wanted to pursue them. During this time at the music collective my hormones were out of whack and my sexual desires had heightened. I had to be on that because I found out earlier in the year that I had endometriosis and would need surgery. Depo Lupron was used to keep me from having a period.

I had an immense amount of passion for this man, but we flirted most of the time because we were working. He was a single father, and I met his son at the job. He was shy around me, but I knew he liked me because he was always joking, flirting, and in my space. He brought a lot of fun into such a nerve wrecking environment. We had to play in front of other people and between my hormones being out of whack and not knowing what the fuck I was doing, I was nervous.

I would make excuses not to play and although true, I didn't even try to push myself. I was happy when I found out I had carpal tunnel and milked it for as long as I could just to get out of playing. Internally I felt shaky and didn't want anyone to see me shaking. I felt confident when playing classical and loved when I was able to leave the jazz room and go play classical music. When my hand wasn't bothering me, this was a joy.

I was in my element. If only I knew back then what I knew now, I would have never done what made me nervous and would have stuck to what made me feel peaceful. Being here was fun and nerve wrecking all at the same time and I don't regret the experience. Being there taught me valuable lessons and boosted my confidence in myself as a violinist.

· · ·

When the summer was over, I still spoke to the guy who flirted with me. We were talking, but not exclusive to each other. He admitted that he liked me and I to him. However, he started becoming distant and not talking to me as much. Months started to go by of me not talking to him and I suspected that he was talking to his baby's mother.

Then, about three months later, he sent me a text message out of the blue asking me to meet him outside my house. It was late at night, and I was elsewhere doing charity work. I had, had enough of his bullshit so I cussed him out and made him aware that he was being disrespectful, and I was not a booty call. I discovered that he saw me as a sexual conquest and not relationship material. I cut him off and never spoke to him again.

Although I was young, I had a strong intuition. I fought my spiritual gifts because I wanted to be normal. My Spirit always gave me an alert when I was going to go overboard and encouraged me to set boundaries. I wasn't naïve for my age because of the wisdom obtained through Spirit. I always knew things when I was younger, but it was dismissed because I was a child. I recall when I was five years old, I would have the same repetitive dream about my father dying from smoking cigarettes. I told my mom about it, and she listened. She was a good listener, but she didn't know about visions at the time and wasn't a spiritual person at all. I felt the need to tell her because those dreams made me sad as a child. My father certainly died three years later from lung cancer. When I was eight years old, I had a dream about the cure for cancer and I told my mom again. She listened, but there was nothing she could really do. She didn't deny what I knew, but she dismissed it and didn't realize I had a gift.

I tried to shut this gift off in high school because I wanted to be this bad, tough girl who refused to be controlled by anyone. I wanted to be free and do whatever my fleshly body told me to do.

When I was sixteen years old and a junior in high school, I was off to a good start. I was doing well in math; I had goals and was focused. However, my friends weren't as close to me as before and I found out that they were doing drugs. We were on different paths, but eventually I got sucked in and started doing drugs as well. I wanted to hang around them and their main focus was drugs, so I went along gave in and went along with them. I had no desire to fit in at school, but when it came to being bored without my friends I gave into temptation. I was never one to skip school, but I did one day to get high. I loved that feeling, but I never felt that same high again.

Every Friday I would go out with my friends and get high. We would smoke blacks, do drugs, and drink beer. During this time my grades started to decline, and I would get cranky when I didn't do drugs. My mom was strict, so I wasn't able to go out when I wanted to and it was hard to hide certain smells from her. The more I started to do drugs the more I started skipping class.

One time she almost caught me because she dropped me off in front of the school. When she left, she saw me across the street with other people. Another time she smelled my glove and it smelled of weed. She asked about it and I lied to her because I didn't want to get my ass whooped.

I wasn't an alcoholic, but my father was. I drank some beer and nothing else, but I would crave alcohol all the time. I had to have it but wasn't able to get it. I started to become addicted to drugs and they became my only focus. I was already on pain meds for endometriosis, and I started abusing those drugs from time to time, along with smoking, and drinking. I would go to school high and not care. If I felt good that was all I cared about.

. . .

One Friday my former friends and I went out. I clearly remember being paranoid that something bad would happen that day. We were smoking and didn't want the cops or anyone to find us. I was high as a kite. We went to the mall, and I picked up some gifts for family. After that we got on the bus and all I remember was being on the bus in a rough neighborhood late at night and laughing uncontrollably. I could see one of my fake ass friends talking to me and saying things that were uncalled for. To this day I don't remember what the fight was about and what she was mad at. I was so high and when I saw her get up, I got up. I had on a heavy suede and fur coat, and I was holding three bags in my left hand. She was arguing and pushed me back a little. Once she did that, I punched her in her head.

I thought the fight would be over, but it continued. She punched me back and I was trying to punch her, but with my left hand while incoherent. I didn't realize until after that there were still three bags in my hand. I grabbed her hair with my right hand then kicked her. In my mind the fight was just beginning. I wanted to get her good and do the best I could while being high, but the bus driver threatened to call the cops on us.

Girls we didn't know came and broke up the fight and someone tried to take my bags so I could hit her, but I didn't trust them. It was a messy night. The girl was twice my size and extremely jealous of how I looked. She was a frenemy for sure and someone I cut off after that. She went around telling people she beat me up, which was a lie. I went to school after that and was fine, but this bothered me because even though she didn't win the fight, I never lost a fight. My toughness was being questioned and I didn't like it. She didn't show up to school for an entire month, but I was ready to whoop her ass at school while I was sober. She wasn't there and I was livid. When she came back, I stepped on her foot by accident, and she didn't open her mouth or make a scene.

Many people didn't believe her, but some people did. I knew the truth and admittedly it wasn't my best fight. However, I didn't get beat up. There were no marks, I was still standing, and I was back in school right after the fracas. People had respect for me because she started with me, and I didn't back down. Some people even brought up how I whooped her ass.

It wasn't a fair fight at all. She was twice my size, I was high and not completely coherent, but I refused to be disrespected. As I got older, I realized that fighting doesn't make you tough, experiences do. I always showed my toughness through anger, rage, and fighting, but toughness came from what I already endured in those sixteen years of life. No one, her included would have been able to survive any of it.

At this time not only was I dealing with drugs, but I was dealing with anorexia and bulimia as well. I remember going to the hairdresser, eating my favorite General Tso Shrimp with yellow fried rice and throwing it up after. Maintaining my weight was important and I had body image issues because adults used to talk about my weight when I was younger. On top of this I was sick.

Dealing with endometriosis took strength. I had so many doctor's visits and blood tests before my surgery that year. When I met with my gynecologist that year, she told me that I would have trouble having children and would need some help. This made me sad. I was so young and told I couldn't have children on my own. Everything hit me when I heard that. Once I found that out I added up all my failures and adversities in life.

. . .

I was disappointed I didn't get in the music school I wanted, I didn't have a father and felt rejected, I was sexually and violently abused when I was younger, the boys I wanted weren't faithful, my last encounter was abusive, and now I'm being told I couldn't have children without help. This made my drug addiction worse, and I started smoking cigarettes. I didn't care about my health because getting pregnant was a dream of mine and now that was gone, I didn't care what I put in my body. I lost my ambitious nature and became a walking depressed sixteen-year-old. Drugs became my best friend and when my family intervened, I didn't listen. My response to them wanting me to stop doing drugs was, "They love me, and I love them." The high from the drugs was the only joy in my life.

I started to envision life differently. I no longer looked to pursue a music career and wanted to be heavy out there in the streets. I believed that my life was meant to be rough, and I was doomed on this earth. I wasn't meant to make it in life. Every time I tried to do something good and go after my goals I was always rejected and not good enough.

Doing drugs took the pain away and made me feel happy without feeling less than. I also felt like I was close to my father when I was high or intoxicated. I tried to understand his life-style through toxic substances. This didn't help me understand him and instead brought me down a dark path. I was trans-forming into an addict who went into a fit of rage from time to time. I used to go into people's classrooms while the teacher was teaching and cuss people out. Another time I tried to stab a girl with my heel of my shoe.

When I was in algebra at school, I remember a girl telling me that my English teacher was talking shit about my presentation. I went upstairs so fast, got in my teacher's face and said, "You said my presentation was shit?" He replied, "No". I went off on him, he looked scared, yet attracted at the same time and then I left the room. I had a feeling my teacher was attracted to me. He would pay a lot of attention to me, make sarcastic jokes and pick on me to get my attention. Many of the girls had a crush on him but I was not one of them. He failed me for that presentation, and I had the choice to redo it and stay after school so he could change my grade or take the D and do a public speaking class next year. I chose to take the D, but thankfully not literally.

Although doing drugs, I was still deeply intuitive, and I remember seeing a movie where the girl stayed after school with her teacher. The teacher raped her. I took that as a sign not to stay after school with my teacher. It didn't feel right, and he already had a crush on me. I followed my Spirit and decided to take the public speaking class next year.

Years later we connected on social media, and I remember him liking my pictures and commenting, 'stunning' underneath one of them. He was strange and dated students once they graduated. He used to flirt with the girls and look at their butt. One of the girls had a word on her pants written across her butt and he read it. I thought that was inappropriate, but he never got fired from his job.

I was upset that I didn't get the best grade in his class, but at least I knew that I would be safe. Speaking of safety, I started going to driving school that year and thoroughly enjoyed it. When we would go on breaks I would go to Dunkin' Donuts and get either a bagel and cream cheese, an egg and cheese croissant, a chocolate glazed donut, or an apple fritter.

At this time, I had a handle on my bulimia and focused more on driving school and positive experiences. I always scheduled the same driver to take me out on the road. He was so cool and loved Hot 93.7, which was and still is a popular radio station.

Poppin' My Collar by Three 6 Mafia was my favorite song to listen to while driving. He was a great instructor and when it was time for me to take the actual driving test I passed. This uplifted my spirits and I felt as if I finally accomplished something. After dealing with a lot of negativity and indulging in negative thinking, which made matters worse, I enjoyed that one positive moment in my life.

I hung onto that positive moment up until I had my laparoscopy surgery for endometriosis. Although small incisions this was major stomach surgery. I was scheduled to have three incisions. I remember being a bit nervous to go under anesthesia, but the doctors made it a comforting experience. When I came out of anesthesia the pain hit.

I felt as though I was hit by a truck and that my bottom half of my body was only connected to my top half of my body through stitches. They put me on the 8th floor where I stayed in a room with a cancer patient. My mom stayed with me every day that I was there but couldn't stay in my room. Four or five doctors came in my hospital room in the morning and looked at my bandages. One of them took off some of the bandages. My mom wasn't happy about that at all because she wasn't able to be in the room, she had no idea who the doctor was, and I was a minor. She spoke to the nurse about it. The nurse, who was about eight or nine months pregnant, was not helpful at all. I was in so much pain and I was given pain meds, but it was still unbearable. She used to give that stare like Debbie Downer on *Saturday Night Live* and I was so irritated with her I wanted a different nurse. The pain was so bad that I couldn't breathe. I'll never forget one night when I was having excruciating pain and I kept pushing the button for a nurse to come. None of the nurses came and I felt helpless. The tears slowly ran down my face and I lay there and cried. Suddenly I saw this bright light and a wing with brown and white feathers.

I was scared and thought I was going to die. The wing caressed my cheek, and I went to sleep. I didn't wake up until the next day. Some of my relatives came to visit me when I was at the hospital and when I came home. When it was time for me to come home, I was escorted out of the hospital in a wheelchair by one of the nursing staff. I was out of school for ten days to recover and when I got back to school I appreciated my life more. Being in the hospital I felt secluded and isolated from the world, so I was thankful to be back in my element. All my teachers except for one miserable bitch of a teacher understood why I missed days of school. I had a doctor's note about my condition, but she tried to give me a hard time about my homework.

She was the worst geometry teacher, and I knew when the school year was over, I wasn't going to miss her. During this time, I was still healing, but able to walk around and didn't have to rest as much. I had to take pain meds in addition to being on hormone replacement medication. The hormone medications prevented me from having a period. Having a period encouraged endometriosis to develop. I was happy about not having a period because they were heavy, I bled a lot and sometimes would have it for two weeks.

I couldn't wear regular pads or tampons like the other girls. I wore thick paper towel pads that made me look as if I had on a diaper. I thought being on these medications would save me from not only have a period but would prevent endometriosis from coming back. Unfortunately, it came back and the gynecologist spotted it. She referred me to another doctor because she had no clue what to do.

I went to see a specialist who was a man. He saw that I had severe endometriosis and scheduled me to have another surgery the following year. I was glad when junior year was over, and I was able to relax. I looked forward to the next year and not having as many classes. During the Summer I met up with a friend and we hung out. We went places we had no business to be in and she used to give me excuses I could tell my mom ahead of time so my mom wouldn't worry.

I remember she had a boyfriend who was in a gang and

facing jail time. Her sister drove us around and brought us to his place. It was a dangerous neighborhood to be visiting late at night. I was in harm's way being with her amongst a gang of boys. One boy I was joking around with pulled a knife on me. He was threatening to cut me with it, but I stood my ground. Even if he was going to cut me with it, I was ready for whatever and was willing to defend myself. He put it away.

Thankfully nothing happened to us, but anything could have happened. This incident did affect me and made me a bit sad years later because someone put a knife close to my face and would have used it. This wasn't the first time someone put a weapon to my face. There was a football game I attended a couple years prior to the knife incident. One of the boys was joking around and put a lighter up to my face and burned my lip.

I didn't think anything of it, but I told him not to do that. I thought it was his character because he was always joking or doing something stupid or dangerous. Another time we got into a physical altercation where he got in my face, I choked him, and he slapped me. My cousin found out about this, and slap boxed with him, slapping the shit out of him.

He never hit me again, but we still didn't get along. Years later in high school we weirdly became friends. I was going through my own toxic behaviors and learning things about myself. We both had secret crushes on each other, and he would hug me frequently in school. No one ever acted on anything. He was my age, and I didn't really deal with boys my age for the simple fact that they were usually interested in light or white girls. I was not one of them.

People saw me as redbone, but I didn't see me like that. A boy I met the previous year and kept in contact with used to call me that. I stayed home from school to meet him at my house but wasn't attracted to him. Nothing happened because the feelings weren't there. I spoke to him on the phone every single day. He was a rapper and wrote a song about me. He even told me that he loved me, but I didn't feel the same way. I spoke to him on the phone and in my mind, I imagined him to look a certain way.

When I met him, and he didn't look how I expected I didn't have feelings for him. My feelings for him started to develop after I met him, and they were light. I cared deeply for him as a friend and could talk to him about anything and everything. He was hot-tempered, but kind and gentle with me. I was sad when he went to prison for his violent temper.

Back when everyone had MySpace I used to put a Free (insert name here) banner for him while he was in jail. This showed my love and support for him as a good friend and potential girlfriend. I kept in contact with his sister and friends to show my loyalty for him. Most of the boys I dealt with were heavy in the streets and this was something that I was accustomed to because being at Hartford all the time I was exposed to the streets.

Some of my family members were involved in that lifestyle and were well known where they're from. I was no stranger to prison, and it didn't make me uncomfortable. The first time I stepped foot into a prison was when I was four years old. I went to visit someone and picked out a necklace in the gift box they had for children. I still remember that peach seashell necklace. It had special meaning at the time, but as I got older, I got rid of it.

I loved getting rid of things and people who no longer served me. When I entered into my senior year of high school at age seventeen, I went in with a cleansed mind, body, spirit, and soul. I wanted to focus on my homework, get serious about my music career, get a car, and get another job. I did skip school from time to time to smoke cigarettes, but I was a changed person from past years.

That year I started lessons with a violin teacher from France. She was the strict teacher from hell, and moody. Learning violin from her was not an enjoyable experience. The energy of my lessons was based on her moods and most of the time she had mood swings. I never knew what mood she was going to be in, and I didn't feel good when it was time for my lessons.

CHAPTER 4

I was still attending the after-school program at the music place at Hartford at this time and a woman there had introduced me to my new violin teacher. I enjoyed playing classical music with the lady at the music place because I knew what I was doing. Eventually I left that program due to not feeling like attending anymore. I continued my lessons with the private studio violin teacher. I was always competitive, but when I became a student of hers, I took it to a new level.

I would go home and look at pieces and their level of difficulty. Then I would compare those pieces with the pieces that I was playing. I would constantly look at levels that people were at and compare myself to that. When I would go to her house for lessons, I was always asking her what level I was at. She gave her honest opinion and although looking back her honest opinion wasn't bad, I took it the wrong way.

Prior to me taking lessons from her and shortly before taking lessons from her I felt ambitious. My ambitious nature led me to audition at one of the top schools for music at Connecticut, which was Hartt School of Music. My nerves got the best of me during that audition, and I remember them telling me to stop playing. They said it as though they were tired of hearing it.

I can laugh at this situation now, but back then I was devastated and felt like my dreams were being crushed. After this audition I thought about trying out again, but I had compared myself to the other seventeen year olds who made it in. When my violin teacher told me that it would be about 1.5 years before I was accepted into Hartt I was mad and disappointed. That feeling of rejection kicked in and I was mad at her, but later realized I was mad at myself.

I was mad at myself for letting my nerves get the best of me. When she said it would take 1.5 years to get into Hartt I heard a waste of time. I also heard, I'll be planning to audition and play everything correctly in lessons then fuck it up when I play for the judges. It felt like a setback because it triggered my insecurities. My insecurities stemmed from not having good teachers for eight years until I met her.

They also stemmed from not wanting to practice because practicing wasn't fun. Practicing wasn't fun when I had no idea what to do. She was the first teacher to give me a practicing routine and showed me how to play with a metronome. I was a seventeen-year-old violinist who felt as if they were playing catch up. Each time I would go home in my 1999 White Ford Escort and practice for a couple to a few days after each lesson with her.

A big accomplishment for me that year was buying my own car. Another accomplishment for me was getting a job at a boarding and grooming place. I loved being around the dogs and cats there but didn't like the manager or assistant manager. The assistant manager irked me more than the manager. Her vibe was an acquired taste that I wasn't trying to sip. I did my work and went home.

I wish people were like animals sometimes. The animals loved me. I would go to school for six periods and was able to leave school early to go to work. That year high school was a breeze. I hung out with a small group of people and stayed focussed. I didn't even make time for a boyfriend that I had. I knew him from middle school, and we were good friends. He moved away for a while, but when he came back to Connecticut, he asked me to be his girlfriend and I said, "Yes".

He wanted to see me, but I was busy with auditions and decided to break it off when I found out he was paying another girl attention. That relationship was short lived, and he went to prison soon after. My intuition was on alert once again with him. My Spirit wouldn't let me spend a lot of time with him. I wasn't one to turn down spending time with a boyfriend, let alone one I knew well. I think at that time I was sick of everybody's shit and needed to be with myself.

When I broke up with him, I came in contact with someone else who I also knew for a long time. We were both alone with each other and he went down my shirt. In the middle of us trying to do something I found out one of my cousin's friends was stabbed to death, so I thought it was inappropriate to continue while the conversation was happening. Our parents were nearby so it didn't go any further than that.

I had a crush on this boy for a long time and vice versa, but we never dated and eventually moved on from one another. We had separated goals and ambitions. He wasn't out in the street or caught up with legal matters. We both wanted to graduate and pursue careers. Someone who had encouraged me to play violin was my favorite orchestra teacher and that same year he died of Leukemia.

Before he passed away someone gave him a violin string that belonged to my violin, which had a sentimental memory attached to it. He started to cry. I missed him when he passed away. He was always jovial, and humor was his middle name.

Knowing that I had a positive teacher to student relationship with my orchestra teacher made me happy. I had no regrets when he died. Graduation was something I looked forward to, but depression hit me like a ton of bricks. I remember driving in my car and feeling nauseous. I felt bored and was sick of my life. I went to Church every Sunday and was a Christian, but I wasn't saved. I didn't receive salvation in my life and felt as though that was the missing piece of the puzzle. I started feeling bad for the lifestyle I was living and had lived and was at a crossroads deciding which way I wanted to go.

I was so unsettled and my guilt regarding everything I had ever done that could be considered, depressed me. The guilt I felt caused horrible insomnia and there were times when I didn't sleep for day. Every last thing I did from the time I was fourteen years old to seventeen years old started to hit me until my conscience couldn't take it anymore. I felt like a hypocrite and even though people knew I wasn't saved, they didn't know what I was doing. No one knew I was hanging out in the street. They knew about the drugs, but thought I stopped. They didn't know about my boyfriends or small sexual encounters I had.

When my mom found out she was mad, but then she got over it. I went through what I know now to be a psychic attack and was heavily tormented. I was the secretary's assistant in the principal's office, and she had made me a black and white necklace to match my black and white dress for graduation. I was thankful, but I didn't enjoy my graduation. I was so unsettled and my guilt regarding everything I had ever done that could be considered depressed me. The happiness I once felt went away and I had horrible insomnia. Some days I couldn't go to sleep. The Pastor, who was also my aunt, prayed I would fall into a deep sleep and I did. That was the first time in a while that I had good sleep. She was a Godsend. As months went by this got better.

. . .

I gave my life to God and got saved. My plans of partying, drinking, and doing drugs were canceled. I got rid of all my friends even the good ones because of that scripture, "Be ye not unequally yoked together with unbelievers..." My friend who I was going to commit to once he got out of prison I left behind. I saw myself having a baby by him and my other older man best friend who went to prison.

I saw myself having a baby by him and also having a baby by my best friend who was older, however, he went to prison. We never had sex but in retrospect if we did have sex when I was fourteen years old, I would have had an eighteen-year-old by now. They were always looking out for my wellbeing and showing me warnings through dreams and visions. I did want to have a baby with the second boy who went to prison because I thought I was meant to be with him, but I turned my life around. He was in a gang and before I gave my life to God, I wanted to be a part of that lifestyle. I wanted to do heavy drugs, be strung out, and so much more. I thought I didn't have a future in music and life in general. Due to my past and my rejection perception I thought the streets were for me.

Church saved my life from going down that path. I'm thankful for my aunt, her biblical teachings, and her prayers. I'm also thankful for my mom for being a listening ear and loving me through everything I went through and being encouraging.

I got accepted into Albertus Magnus College for Psychology but couldn't afford to attend. I was not an honor roll student in high school, so I would have been under close advisement, but this filled me with joy and gratitude. Finally, I got an acceptance letter from a school I actually wanted to attend and this filled my heart with joy and gratitude.

My Psychology teacher was proud of me. He was a great teacher who used to have us meditate in his class. I felt peaceful after. I was excited about college, but I didn't want to go to college. I preferred to stay home and run my own business. I had my own oil business where people would make oils that smelled like designer perfume. I would sell Juicy Couture, Marc Jacobs, Ralph Lauren Blue, and more to people from school and people at Church. Everyone loved it because it was an inexpensive option in comparison to the perfume. I loved selling items and being a vendor at the hair salon I went to. Entrepreneurship was something I looked into but was frowned upon and misunderstood. I thought being an entrepreneur was someone who didn't know what they were doing in life and went with the flow. I had health issues and being an entrepreneur wasn't feasible at the time.

That summer before I entered college, I had my second laparoscopy surgery for endometriosis. I met with the specialist at another hospital and when I got there him, his daughter who was also a doctor and another one of my gynecologists, plus a nurse was there. They gave me the rundown of how the surgery was going to go and prepped me for it. As the nurse was doing my IV, I noticed the she had a funny smell on her breath. I noticed she was a bit off and smelled of alcohol. What happened next was shocking. After she stuck a needle in my arm I was wheeled off into surgery. I was given anesthesia and as I'm going under, I could hear people yelling frantically. It was too late because I went under.

When I came to I saw a huge arm that looked like it should have been on a person who weighed at least 400 lbs. I was panicking and the doctor told me what happened. He told me that the nurse who was supposed to do the IV stuck me in my cartilage. He told me after they gave me the anesthesia my arm was swelling rapidly and was even bigger than it was. I only weighed 135 lbs. and had an arm of a 400 lb. woman on me. They were able to get the swelling to come down and thankfully I was okay. My arm hurt very badly due to the pain from the four incisions they had to make. The doctor also informed me that the endometriosis had severely damaged my appendix, so they took it out. I had Stage IV endometriosis, so it was a good thing I had health insurance.

I needed health insurance, so to Manchester Community College I went. I signed up last minute because I only applied to one college and didn't want to go anywhere else. I got into Manchester Community College and went for my Associates Degree in the Arts. This was an incredibly peaceful and fun experience. I finally felt the peace that passed all understanding.

Once again, I reinvented myself and started fresh. I always changed my hair color and I recall having my hairdresser dye the bottom half of my hair dark brown and the top half light blonde. I wore it straight and curly. I dressed nicely at all times, but I was even more classy and elegant. I stopped swearing, I stopped engaging in drama, and disappeared from everyone to focus on my college career. Meeting new people in the same career field was refreshing and I felt like an independent adult. I had about four to five classes per semester and was getting A and B grades in school. I had time to rest and focus on my mental, emotional, physical, and spiritual health. It was the change I needed.

When I wasn't at school I would be working at the boarding and grooming place, selling my oils, going shopping at the mall or going to eat at Starbucks, Dominos, Wendy's, Burger King, and other fast-food restaurants. I also went to the hairdresser in the mornings because I didn't have classes then.

One day in the winter when I was leaving the hairdresser in my car, I felt someone hit me. She hit the bumper of my car. We exchanged insurance info and I had all her car information. For someone who had just hit someone she was very rude and nonchalant about it. I declined the ambulance, but later on that night I regretted that decision.

I woke up with excruciating pain and was screaming. My mom was there to help me through this difficult time. I had pain all over my back and had trouble sleeping. Shortly after I decided to go connect with a lawyer and sue her. The case went on for about three years. My first lawyer was dreadful, he was lazy and sounded as though he was siding with the lady.

To this day I don't know what was wrong with that poor excuse of a lawyer. The amount that he said my accident was worth was a slap in the face. I had to go to physical therapy every week for an entire year and I wasn't able to use my left arm to play violin at school. It impaired my life and my ability to put in the maximum effort into my instrument.

He made everything worse by questioning me, mixing up the story because he wasn't doing his job, and adding more stress. I had to go through the court system to have him removed from my case because he refused. One of my cousins came with me as a support because I had gone through so much with him. I got him removed and was relieved. It was a great day.

One of my family members referred me to another lawyer who helped her previously. This one was so much better than the last. He was determined to win, and we did win. I got four times the amount the other lawyer was trying to get and was grateful to the new lawyer. Besides the injury that impacted me, my life seemed to go back to normal.

I prayed daily, attended Bible Studies, and focused on my homework. I enjoyed school because I learned new things and loved being around different people from different areas. No one knew one another. People were peaceful and mature.

My mom and I used to have a peaceful relationship until I got older and started college when our relationship became tumultuous and extremely volatile. I wanted to live by myself and tried to move when I was in high school but was discouraged from doing so because of where I was at in my life. I wasn't making the best decisions and my plans to stay in New York were not the greatest. I wanted to be on my own for a while. Once I was older and had a mind of my own, I didn't want to do what she told me.

She was raised in a household where everyone was hit when they did something wrong. She never looked at it as abuse, but I saw it that way. I constantly forgave her because I was heavily into Church, and we were taught about forgiveness. Family members did have to intervene on numerous occasions to mediate between my mom and me.

I was known to cut people off with no remorse so it was rough having to stay with someone who I so badly wanted to get away from but couldn't. I felt free when I went to school, but not when I came home.

We had many good days, which I appreciated. I loved to laugh with her and order food from various restaurants. We would watch our favorite shows together. She was there for me but would get into these angry moods as did I.

It was hard to elevate and work on my spiritual journey being around my mom. We discussed how I was feeling multiple times but couldn't see eye to eye. I talked to her about this after the incident and she told me that it wasn't intentional to be mean to me as I was elevating.

I tried many times to show her this pattern of always being mean when I was elevating. She denied it and said it wasn't her intent. I believed her because she was always there for me and very supportive. My mom had a history of taking up for me, bringing me to all of my doctor's visits, taking care of me, and coming to all of my concerts.

We didn't have the best relationship, but I couldn't fault her for everything. I wish things would have been different between us, but that's the way it was at times. She loved the concerts and I loved when she came to watch me perform. I enjoyed the concerts at Manchester Community College. One of my favorite performances was at a wine tasting event. It was a small chamber orchestra of three people and we played beautifully.

After that performance we got to go around and sample free food that the culinary students made. It was so good, and I made sure to make my rounds to every table. Another one of my favorite performances was at an art gallery. It was an intimate setting at a peaceful place. The people were pleasant, and we had fun playing Bach.

Before I finished college, I found out that one of my aunts who was my best friend and second mama had pancreatic cancer. I was devastated and almost passed out. Once I found out I spent almost every day with her. I made sure she laughed, and we had fun together. I wanted to be there for her every step of the way because I loved her very much and because she was always there for me.

My mom took her to her chemotherapy treatments. One day my aunt asked me to come with them as she took her chemotherapy treatments. My mom didn't want me to go because I was extremely close to my aunt and it was depressing. She wanted to protect me from being sad. During the springtime of my second year at college I received a phone call that my aunt was taken to the hospital. She was admitted because she wasn't feeling well. Some of my family and I spent every day at the hospital with her. We never left her alone with any doctors or nurses. Everyone who was there took turns while she was there. I couldn't sleep and was beyond depressed about this. I had just auditioned to get my Bachelor of Science degree in Music Education at Central Connecticut State University. I made it in and besides my mom my aunt was my biggest cheerleader.

When she was coherent, I told her and her response was, "Why wouldn't you?" She always believed in me and loved when I played the violin. I performed violin in church since I was eleven years old, and she was always in the front cheering me on. When I told her I made it into another great music school at Connecticut she had a beautiful smile on her face.

I hated seeing her in pain and suffering in the hospital. It wasn't fair and she didn't deserve it. She was the most supportive person. On my last birthday before she went to the hospital, she made sure she took me out to a restaurant. I told her that she didn't have to, but she insisted. I picked her up because she wasn't able to drive during this time. It was just she and I who went to Ruby Tuesday's and we both went to the salad bar first.

She became very weak, and I saw her struggling, so I helped her get her food. It was difficult to watch her having a hard time. She was such a strong, vibrant woman. I still saw her that way but knew that she wasn't in the best of health. When she went to the hospital she had to be on heavy medications.

Some days she was coherent, but most of the time she wasn't. It saddened me to see her this way because I wanted to hear her voice and wanted to know that she would be okay. One of the dumb ass nurses walked into her room and pissed me the fuck off with what she said. My mom, some relatives, and I were in the room that day the nurse walked in.

Someone mentioned that they were going to see my aunt Wednesday and the nurse said, "If she's here Wednesday." I angrily said, "She'll be here." My aunt knew that I was blunt and feisty as she was. I was holding her hand as I was talking to the nurse. She turned to me and smiled. I was overjoyed to see her smiling and it gave me hope that she would make it.

I had no doubt she would get better. I took some time off school, but my mom had encouraged me to go to school that next Wednesday. It was my last year of college, but I didn't want to leave her, and I didn't care if I graduated or not. Family came first and she was my first priority.

Despite this, I listened to my mom, went to school, and did my last performance. That same week I had fired my private lesson teacher because we didn't see eye to eye, and I was tired of her mood swings. I played an extremely difficult piece by Bach and once I was finished, I found out that my aunt had passed away. Guilt and regret immediately hit me. She had passed away the only day that I wasn't there. I wanted to come up there as she lay in the hospital bed after the last breath left her body.

My mom told me not to come because I was close to my aunt, and it would have pushed me over the edge even more. That was the hardest day of my life and I felt as though my heart was ripped out of my chest. I cried uncontrollably and was inconsolable. I wanted to be in the casket with her and couldn't bear living without her. I had no clue how I was going to navigate life without her.

I was so angry she left this earth so soon and mad that a kind and loyal soul had to suffer so badly. I wouldn't wish that on most people. She was a strong warrior who put up with a lot of pain. The only comforting thought was that she was no longer in pain. On the day of her funeral, I couldn't cry. I cried for days and hours that when it was time for the funeral I was all cried out. I had school so I wasn't able to go to the family viewing the day before, but one of my cousin's showed me a photo of her. She looked absolutely beautiful.

The funeral was closed casket and it was a lovely service. I went to her burial and stayed next to her casket while everyone left to greet one another. Although she was gone, I didn't want to leave her. It took me years to get over her death and occasionally I still cry. She was a rare soul that no one could ever be like, and I will forever love and miss her. Thank you so much auntie for making my life the most joyous, happiest place. Thank you for the wonderful memories. I'll love you always.

Life was different and being in school for the last two months was depressing. It was time for graduation, and it was a better day than the previous. I spent about two years at Manchester Community College and graduated with a 3.75 GPA. I was always on the Dean's List and received a scholarship for that. Several relatives, my mom included, attended my graduation where I received my Associates Degree in the Arts. They did a great job putting together the graduation in that spacious auditorium.

I had three months off then I was headed to Central Connecticut State University to start working on my Bachelor of Science degree in Music Education. At this time, I was working at another place where I was in close proximity to dogs and cats. This was a veterinary hospital.

I quit the other job because they cut back on my hours. At first, I loved working there, but as time went on I noticed that management sucked, the employees talked about each other all the time, and the rules and regulations made the job feel like prison.

On Labor Day in September 2009, I was nineteen years old and on my way to work in my purple and white scrub clothes. My hair was black at the time, and I weighed around 160 lbs. Before I left the house, I had an eerie feeling and I couldn't put my finger on it.

I felt as though something bad was going to happen. Surprisingly I had a great day at work. This was odd because I hated going to work and we actually had fun that day. I got in my car and thought maybe that was just a feeling that came and went.

When I left work, I went to Goldberg's Bakery. I was still a vegetarian and I loved their egg and cheese bagels. That day I got extra egg and extra cheese on my bagel. I couldn't wait to get in the car and eat it. When I got in the car I started driving and eating my bagel. Before I could take a bite, the light turned green and a car came out of nowhere. It turns out the woman went through a red light when she should have stopped.

I ended up hitting her on the right side of her car. It was a T-bone accident. As she was driving across the road all I remember saying was, "No!!!" I felt something hard as steel hit me in the mouth and after that I woke up to see smoke. My head came up off of the dashboard. I could see the airbags deployed and was completely out of it.

I noticed that I was locked in the car and for sure thought that the car was going to blow up and I was going to die. For a minute I was afraid, but then I asked God to forgive me of my sins and thought, "I'll be with my aunt who passed away again." The minute I said that an angel placed my finger on the button to let the window down. I quickly jumped out of the car.

The cops came and the ambulance. Two men in an ambulance took me to the hospital. One of the men thought my arm was broken. It was red, purple, and blue because I had burned it. The heat from the airbag had caused the damage and it hurt very badly. My knee was also in pain. I couldn't talk that well and sounded very much like the lady who lost her voice in the movie *US* by Jordan Peele.

The reality was if I had stayed in that car a bit longer, I would have died from smoke inhalation. I was doped up on Morphine to deal with the pain. I called my mom to let her know what happened, so she called a friend to take her to the hospital to see me. I stayed there for the day, and they let me go home. Before we went home, we went to go see the car. The car was totaled, and my mom had to get another car afterwards.

I once again had to sue. This case took about two years and was stressful, but this time I had a good "lawyer". It was the same "lawyer" that won my last car accident case. We won this case as well and it was a relief. I had to go to an orthopedic doctor and to physical therapy for 1.5 years for that accident. Looking back, I don't know how I put up with so much stress. I was still grieving over my aunt that passed away and mentally I wasn't well. Although I was in pain from the car accident, I was happy because there was a possibility that I didn't have to go to Central Connecticut State University.

CHAPTER 5

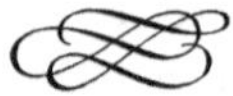

I wasn't in the right frame of mind to handle a rigorous music program. I needed time off but was unable to. I was still using prescription drugs to cope with life. I wanted to process my emotions after two consecutive traumatic experiences. That fucking health insurance is what made me go to school with severe injuries. I was still sick with endometriosis and was on various medications for it. I was on the IUD, Norethindrone, Loestrin, Yaz, Depo Lupron, Oxycodone, Hydrocodone, Ibuprofen, estradiol, and two others. These were supposed to prevent me from having a period and from endometriosis coming back. I also took these for pain and was on all of these in a rotation since I was fifteen, I started to become addicted to these when I was sixteen and it lasted until I was in my twenties in college. My mom had me taken off the Hydrocodone when I was 16 because I was addicted. I would nod off and see bunnies and rainbows. The rest of the meds I took in rotation for years. Out of all the hormone replacement meds I hated the Yaz, Depo Lupron, and Norethindrone. The side effects were horrendous. I started off at Manchester

Community College weighing 135 lbs. and within three months I weighed 168 lbs. This put me in a depression. School was fun, but I felt uncomfortable in my body and my self-esteem was shot for the most part. When I was on the Depo Lupron, I had a high sex drive and hot flashes. I wasn't having sex because I was celibate being in the Church so there was no sexual activity. I felt like I was going through menopause. The side effects from Norethindrone trump all of them. One of the side effects was suicidal thoughts and that's exactly what I had. I would be in physics class doing my work and then suddenly, a feeling of dread, darkness, and depression would come over me. I didn't think I had anything to live for. I told my mom about this and then my doctor. Thankfully, he took me off it and I gradually went back to normal.

I was able to lose 10 lbs. before I started back at Central Connecticut State University but wanted to lose a lot more. On my first day of college there one of my cousin's brought me to school because I couldn't drive. I was severely injured and needed extra assistance. I should have been resting but had to sacrifice my physical health and mental well-being during this time to keep my health insurance. My arm was burned badly, I could barely walk, or talk. I went from taking 4-5 classes at Manchester Community College to taking 11 classes per semester at Central Connecticut State University. Over-whelmed wasn't the word for what I was experiencing. I was still working at the veterinary hospital but took time off. That would have been overkill for me if I was still working during this time. We already got homework on the first day and the professors showed no mercy.

I was used to volunteering in class at Manchester Commu-nity College. I loved to participate, be outspoken, and in the forefront. I wanted to transfer that same behavior over to Central Connecticut State University. I was a student who excelled so I thought this would be the same for me at my new college. However, I decided to sing in aural skills with a throat that was healing from smoke inhalation from the car accident. This was not wise of me to do, but I refused to be put in the background and loved to be bold. When I tried singing, I failed miserably.

I received a 3 out of 10 and was instantly depressed. I felt like a failure and even asked my teacher if I could try it again. There were no second chances. This was a big change from the first college I went to, and I was devastated. It took time to get over the fact that on my first day of school I failed in front of other people. The professor showed no remorse. This was common amongst all the professors. When I walked into piano class and told my piano teacher that I was in a car accident and couldn't play, she didn't ask how I was feeling. She simply told me to play with my left hand instead. This was an awful start to the school year, but I hung in there and never gave up. I was very observant and watched how they treated the students. I started to mimic back this attitude and put my emotions to the side. I realized I had to play their game if I was going to survive this music program. When I was home, I let my emotions out, but at school I showed nothing. When my first week of school was over, I received an email from the Aural Skills teacher recommending that I get extra help from her. This was a blow to my ego because I never needed extra help in college.

I declined the help and tried to do it on my own. At the time I thought the professor was mean and out to get me as she gave me a bad grade. Telling her I was just in a car accident didn't move her from her stance. I regretted volunteering and shouldn't have sung, but I expected her to understand. This made me reject her help and get into a competitive mindset where I had to prove something to her. I thought I could devote a small amount of practice time at home into this Aural Skills class and get good grades. This wasn't so and I saw that I was still failing. Sometimes I performed well, but most times I performed poorly. This was a change from the community college. I felt as though I had the Midas touch there but here, I felt powerless and out of place.

I had a knack for music theory and always achieved success in that class. My other classes were extremely difficult, but I received good grades. The only class I felt hopeless in was Aural Skills and that bothered me. I was not a fan of The teacher's style and felt as though I was teaching myself and was on my own for the first year of being in her class.

Music Education was a rigorous major, almost like a double major. There was the music portion of it and the education portion of it. Both required mastery and outstanding grades to go to the next level. You had to get a C and above or a B and above to pass the class. The only class I had to repeat was Aural Skills, but many students had to repeat that class.

You had to rely solely on your ear to sing. I knew how to sing, and she liked my voice, however, we had to read notes to sing in a random key that she gave us. We also couldn't pick what exercise from the book we wanted to sing. People went to school for singing and failed that class. I had to sing in other classes, but it was much different from that class. My other classes were music history, orchestra, chamber orchestra, private lessons, music technology, performance-based classes, and education classes.

My entire life was devoted to music education. Everything was time consuming. Between practicing for performances, preparing for tests, presentations, and music tech I had no time for anything else. I was glad I was accepted into this school to pursue a career in music, but I didn't have a say in what my schedule would look like. Almost none of my credits transferred over from the first college so I was starting from scratch.

Although this took a toll on my mental health I didn't give up. If I had to do it all over again I wouldn't because mental health comes first, but I'm grateful for the life lessons, discipline, and education under my belt that I utilize in my life today. I saw people dropping out left and right. They couldn't handle the pressure of a rigorous program. If I had to describe the music education program as a movie it would be *Hunger Games* for sure.

Each semester I had to do at least 4 violin recitals. The composers that I frequently played was Bach, Handel, Mozart, Vivaldi, Jules Massenet, Brahms, and Prokofiev. One of my best performances were playing *Meditation de Thais* by Jules Massenet. I remember playing it in front of my private lesson teacher and the accompanying pianist at one of the last rehearsals before the final performance. My teacher who was a professional violin player in a popular symphony at Hartford started crying. She thought it was absolutely beautiful. I was not one to get nervous when performing. I frequently performed in church, at schools, and on stages for most of my life. Sometimes I would be nervous and had a few bad performances that are cringe worthy. For the most part I loved to perform and express what I worked so hard on.

As a performer I had to do what was called a jury. I had to prepare two different pieces, twice per semester and play in front of judges. They judged intonation, melodic interpretation, and more. Most juries I received a B as a grade and nothing below that. One jury I received a C as a grade, and I was so pissed at myself. I was ready for my performance, and I overly prepared the piece. I was ready to do my last jury and go out with a bang and wasn't a bit nervous.

Energy transfer is real, and this is one of the incidents where I absorbed someone else's energy. I remember waiting to go into the room of the jury very excited to perform. A student walked in nervous as fucking hell. She performed well, but when it was my turn to perform my bow was shaking and I was so nervous. My violin teacher recommended I take beta-blockers after that performance. She was concerned that something was wrong.

That was one of my first lessons on how to observe energy and not absorb it. I also didn't know that at the time I had undiagnosed Ataxia and Familial Hemiplegic Migraine Type 1, which would also explain the bow shaking. With Ataxia people tend to have tremors. I discovered this ailment years later, but wish I knew about it earlier because it would have made me feel better about some of my performances.

Leave it up to food to make me feel better. Central Connecticut State University had the best food. I would get their quesadillas, French fries, and pizza. It was so satisfying. Other food places that I loved were Tony's Pizzeria and Underground Deli. Those two places were my favorite. I loved a good grinder with coleslaw and French fries. It was comfort food. Ruby Tuesday's Shrimp Sampler was also a favorite amongst my mom and me.

After dinner each night I would take a bath and I started noticing certain scarring on my body that looked like a melanoma. I thought I had cancer. My mom was certain that I had cancer as well. I was bleeding a lot out of my rectum, and I was very tired. I had a hole in my rectal area with yellow gunk coming out of it. I itched so badly and wore plastic around that area so I could go to sleep. I got no relief whatsoever and went to a doctor in the area who was nonchalant. She gave me an itch cream that made it worse. I felt sick and gross, like my life was over and had no idea what was going on. Tests were taken at the doctor's office that showed no sign of cancer, but I had all of the symptoms. A couple years previously I lost skin in the middle of my breast area. Two small balls had burst and my skin dissolved. I bled there and itched as well. I thought I had breast cancer. After meeting with that nonchalant doctor my mom and I switched over from vegetarian to vegan.

She was trying to lose weight and so was I. After I made the switch, my symptoms started to improve. I started to feel better and there were no signs of itching and bleeding. My mom was 360 lbs. and started losing weight fast eating a plant-based vegan diet. I was so proud of her. She was always supportive of me and I of her.

She never missed a performance unless I played during the day while she was at work. I recall her only missing two out of at least twenty plus performances. Walking was difficult for her when she was heavier. I used to feel so bad when I would see her sweat as she walked to the auditorium where I performed. She also never missed a celebration. I was frequently on the Dean's List at school, accepted into Kappa Delta Pi, and an integral part of the Dean's Leadership Institute. I got various scholarships and was invited to a banquet dinner. My mom and an uncle came to support.

I enjoyed being in the Dean's Leadership Institute and worked closely with the Interim Associate Dean in the School of Education and Professional Studies. She told me that I inspired the program and that my personality would suit me in my career as a teacher.

She saw leadership qualities in me and encouraged me to get my Masters in Educational Leadership. The education department was my favorite place to be. All of the music classes were in Welte Hall, so it was refreshing to be in another building and meet other people who weren't in my major. By this time, I had cleaned up my act and wasn't using prescription drugs to cope with my life and past traumas. I used to use them to go to sleep when I would have flashbacks of abuse. Changing my diet and progressing in life made me quit cold turkey.

It was as if I got out of solitary confinement when I would go to the education department. I adored the professors in that department. They were much different from the music professors. Granted I was at Central Connecticut State University for 3.5 years, which was outstanding and by then I was used to all the music professors and their personalities. Most people stayed there for 5-6 years because of how difficult it was. The professors in the School of Education and Professional Studies were more empathetic and reminded me of some of the teachers back at Manchester Community College.

One professor was an absolute sweetheart. He taught Special Education. As a future music education teacher, I had to take a variety of education classes to be able to teach pre-K-12 students. Learning about how to teach Special Education students warmed my heart.

I knew those students had specific challenges and needed to be taught in a plethora of different ways. When I was injured and had carpal tunnel, he showed leniency with my assignment due dates. I appreciated him for that because I was left-handed, and my left arm and hand were both injured. At this time, I was unable to play violin and I expressed that to my orchestra teacher. She wasn't too happy about that and wanted me to sit in the back. She didn't ask me how I felt and instead thought it was disconcerting to be sitting in the front during a performance. I was mad at her, but my angels told me not to say anything to her. I told my private lesson teacher what she said, and she had a talk with the orchestra teacher.

About one week later the same orchestra teacher came up to me and told me that her daughter got her hand slammed in a window and almost wasn't able to do her cello audition. After that she was kind to me and let me sit in the front. Karma is real and treating people with kindness goes a long way.

I played second violin for a bit because she needed someone to lead that section, but usually played in the first violin section.

I remember preparing to audition for first violin, practicing every day until the piece I performed was perfect. The orchestra teacher acknowledged how well I played and put me in first chair of the first violin section. This was another huge accomplishment as I was able to play with one of the top violinists. She and I bumped heads from time to time and got into an argument. We both had strong personalities, but eventually we started to get along great with each other.

When I wasn't at school, I was preparing for another performance at various churches my Pastor preached at. Before the Church service started, I would play to set the atmosphere and get rid of low vibrational entities also known as demons. In 2010 when I was twenty-one years old, I started doing my Field Experiences teaching. I was excited to go to schools, observe the teachers and students, and teach as well.

As much as I was excited, I was also antsy because I wanted to take over the class. It was a lovely change to travel to different schools and not be stuck at college every day. When I was twenty-two years old and it was time for student teaching it was the happiest day of my life. Everyone had to be accepted to do student teaching, so this was another win for me. In order to even be accepted into student teaching you had to be accepted into the School of Educational Leadership and Professional Studies. Before I was able to get in, I had to pass a rigorous test in the music department. Most people failed this, and I did the first time. Because most people failed, we all were able to take it again. When I took the test again, I passed with flying colors. The test consisted of aural skills, theory, piano and more.

I nailed the aural skills portion, and my ear was so advanced that my intonation was impeccable. I even modulated to another key and sang the notes flawlessly. How ironic that my Aural Skills teacher became one of my favorites when I was almost out of school. She wanted me to pass the test. You would have thought I had perfect pitch. When I received my grades for this test and my acceptance letter I felt as though I was getting closer to my dreams. I was accepted to student teach at two schools. One school was an elementary school at New Britain, Connecticut and the other school was a middle school at Simsbury, Connecticut.

By this time, I had quit my job at the veterinary hospital because there were fake women who worked there that were trying to get me fired. Between getting in a car accident back in 2009, having to wear a leg brace, and not walking as great as I used to, I had to sit down a lot. The doctor there didn't like people sitting down so there was only one chair. The women were mad that I had to sit down due to my injury. They reported me to the Office Manager. I didn't wait for anyone to fire me. I quit because I was already getting into arguments with the managers there. I checked them for trying to talk to me rudely.

I was happy to leave that job and don't recommend anyone work there. The management and the doctor sucked. The doctor who was the boss sexually harassed some of the workers with physical touch. He never sexually harassed me and wouldn't because I put him in check before as well. My future looked brighter while the people there were stuck in the same horrible job that paid a little bit of nothing.

Sometimes success is the best revenge, and the level up is people's karma. I was excited once I got out of school and was able to do full-time student teaching. The summer before this one was pretty rough. I struggled with transmuting energies and had no clue how to do that. I recall picking up on the energy of someone that I walked by, and it was dark. After that I went from feeling peaceful to feeling tormented in mind, body, spirit, and soul. I didn't sleep for an entire year.

I didn't know how to observe and not absorb energy. My mom taught me how to do this, but it took me time to grasp. This was so bad. Dark entities and otherworldly creatures of the dark forces invaded thoughts and surrounded me. I didn't feel like my jovial self. I made it to the finish line and here came these dark forces.

This took time to get rid of and a variety of techniques and only I was able to do so. My aunt, who was my Pastor as well, prayed for me, she hugged me, and encouraged me. She made my birthday special that year and I loved her for it.

My mom didn't think I was crazy. She listened to me, hugged me, and gave me her support. However, they couldn't be with me 24/7. I had to do the work. I knew the mind was a battlefield and other people couldn't win my war.

I said scriptures throughout the entire day until I felt peace. This wasn't fair that I had to do this all day, but it worked. Doing this reminded me of the boy in Stephen King's *It* where he would say the names of the birds for 'It' to go away. My mom gave me wise counsel and told me what to do with my thoughts and where to place them. I tried everything.

I soon recognized if I wanted to see change then I had to put the work in. In fairness, learning the lesson is what allowed me to pass my spiritual test. I conquered the dark forces and going into Student Teaching with a clear head felt great. I remember going shopping for all my teacher clothes. That was an enjoyable experience. My favorite places to shop for teaching outfits were Ann Taylor Loft and Banana Republic. They had the best outfits.

The first teacher for my student teaching experience at one of the elementary schools at New Britain, Connecticut was a kind and rare gem. We immediately clicked. She taught general music to K-5 and told me to observe her for the first three weeks. I watched her very carefully and when it was my turn to teach, I was a pro. The teachers and the principal loved me. The music teacher and I would always laugh and have lunch together. We had a special bond that I can't explain. I still have a video on my computer of her talking to one of the paraprofessionals at the school. They were complimenting my teaching style and how great I was.

I keep this video because it was the long-lasting memory that I would have of her. Within one month someone discovered her unconscious in her home and took her to the hospital. I was able to visit her when she was there. She was unresponsive, but she could still hear. She loved my voice, so I sang to her. About a week later she passed away. Her funeral was sad, and I cried. I will always remember her and the special connection we had. She always encouraged me and made me feel as though I was more than enough. I am forever grateful for her. My final grade in Student Teaching with her was an A-. My school mentor ,who came to observe me each time I taught, gave me that final grade. That same mentor also warned me about my next teacher. Apparently, the next teacher had a strong personality and was often considered rude.

I didn't think that teacher would be rude to me, but I kept what I'd been told in the back of my mind. Next month I met this teacher and she looked like a lady I saw in a vision. The Spirit realm had warned me about her. I was awakened by a vision of her, and it flashed in front of my eyes while they were open. Whenever anything flashes in front of my eyes like that it's a warning. I knew something was off about her when I met her. She was in her early thirties. During this time, I had two new mentors that worked in the music department. One was a general music professor and the other was an instrument professor.

The general music professor met with the student teacher and me. He told her that I recently experienced the death of a teacher. She wasn't sympathetic to that, and this was her first time having a student teacher. She expressed to the professor that she wanted me to be in charge and take the reins. This was code for she didn't know what the fuck she was doing and was too arrogant to say so.

I hated every single day that I had to be around her. When she introduced me to the other teachers at the school and someone said I was beautiful I'll never forget that fake ass smile on her face. It hurt her entire soul to hear someone showing people other than her attention. My lesson plans were never good enough for her and she didn't take the time to show me in detail what she wanted me to do.

The other music teacher at the school in New Britain always loved my lesson plans, but this teacher at Simsbury put me through the ringer. I used to be up all night writing lesson plans. Usually, a lesson plan should be 1-3 pages max. My lesson plans for orchestra and ensembles were 7 pages. When I would show her the finished product, she complained about it.

Her emails to me were always rude and belittling. My professors knew me as an outspoken, strong-willed person and told me not to say anything to her. However, I didn't heed their advice the first time and let it be known that she was being disrespectful to me. She became dramatic and stormed out of the room after telling me that it was like a brick wall, and she couldn't get in. She also said she was leaving before she said anything disrespectful.

I was off to a bad start with her, and the days got worse. I wasn't sleeping well because I was under so much stress working with her. She wanted me to know what I was doing without showing me what to do. Even when I asked questions, she was rude. My time was spent reaching out to other teachers to learn how to play various instruments that I wasn't taught in school and studying as much as I could.

Although I went to school for violin, we were not taught

how to teach it to other students. When I went for student teaching, she was unwilling to help me and instead made my life miserable. If she were anyone else, I would have yelled at her and went in a fit of rage, but due to the fact that this was my last hoorah before graduation I bit my tongue. I was too stressed to eat at lunch with her like I was in the beginning because she constantly had me working and never helped me. She would accuse me of being anorexic because I was losing weight.

I recall going out to eat with all the teachers and she drove another teacher and I in the same car. I ate all my food, but she saved hers and said, "My grandmother used to tell me that it was ladylike to save my food when I went out to eat." All I was thinking was, Bitch who gives a fuck about what your grandmother has to say. I like to eat so shut the fuck up asshole. I was in the Church and had to graduate so I never got the chance to say that, but if she pulled that shit now, I would have left her shitting in her pants and in tears.

I requested multiple times to be removed from that student teaching placement. I felt as though my own professors started to turn on me. That student teacher was very manipulative and charming. They wanted to fit in with her and were scared so they took up for her.

One of them even got the same engagement ring she had on. I thought weird as fuck. I felt as if I was in the Twilight Zone. One day the student teacher sent me a text and told me that she wouldn't be at school during first period because she had to clean her house. I let my professors know and they thought that she was valid in missing school that day.

It was mind-blowing to see how two-faced they were. They knew she was an evil asshole, but then sided with her. They refused to remove me, and I was stuck there with her. I used to cry out of sheer rage because I couldn't punch her in the face.

When I got to school, she had pissed me off for the last time. She said something that ticked me off and I went in full whiteout mode. I was used to blacking out in the past and having to attend anger management, but this was new to me. Whiteout mode was seeing everything and everyone around me, but being zoned out, feeling calm, but ready to do harm all at the same time.

I reached my breaking point with her verbal abuse on a weekly basis and her physical abuse when she snatched the violin from underneath my neck. I saw myself take her entire body out of her chair and throw it through the glass window. It made me happy, and I didn't care about the consequences because no one was helping me out of this horrible situation. The only thing that stopped me was a phone call from my mom. She told me not to do anything.

Weirdly the next day I decided to send a text to my mom while I was at school to tell her, "I feel like I'm going to explode." Unbeknownst to me the text went to the student teacher. I didn't mean to do that, but God makes no mistakes. That had to happen.

She called my professors and was scared for her life so I got my wish to leave the assignment. I went out with a bang. Before I left, I conducted the 7th and 8th grade orchestra beautifully. I recall a couple times her complimenting my playing, which showed that she was a jealous bitch who saw someone beautiful and talented.

I was so glad to be removed from that assignment. She gave me an F, but my professors moved me to a new, fun, and exciting teacher. He was very cool. They changed my grade from an F to a C and I graduated with no issues.

After graduation I went to look for a private violin teacher job at Simsbury in the area. I wasn't able to work in the schools quite yet because I had to go for my certification testing. The owner hired me. However, the evil student teacher knew the owner and found out that I would be working there.She told the parents of my potential violin students that I was a horrible teacher. The owner conveyed this to me, gave me a viola as a parting gift, and told me that it wasn't in my best interest to work there. He didn't like the student teacher I had and said she was jealous of me and wasn't rhythmically inclined. I also found out that allegedly she had a relationship in the past with an under aged boy.

She had some serious issues that she didn't deal with. People thought she was crazy but was scared of her. I was not one to kiss her ass and spoke up to her. She didn't like it then she got scared when I said I was going to blow up. It made me chuckle inside.

I went on to be a permanent sub at a school on the North End of Hartford. I loved that school and the students. I prepared them for their performance and taught them how to read music. When that job was over, I took the Praxis test to become certified three different times until I passed. Nothing that we learned in school was on that test and I felt relieved when I passed. I was not certified and able to teach in the schools until then.

The process for hiring music teachers was different from hiring regular elementary, middle school, or high school teachers. Several months later I went to audition at a high school in Manchester, Connecticut. They loved my audition and put me through to the next round where they had me teaching an orchestra class. Other people auditioned for that teaching spot but didn't make it through. A popular teacher from Farmington and I were the last teachers to be accepted for one spot. He was considered one of the top string teachers and was much older than I was.

He got the job, but this boosted my confidence as a strings

teacher. I knew I was capable of teaching students and didn't let that evil bitch of a student teacher's negative words stop me. Summer was ending and I started to panic.

My dream job was to work at Manchester where my maternal grandmother used to live. It was so peaceful and quiet there. Most of the music jobs were occupied. I just so happened to see an opening in New Britain for a violin teacher. I was hired on the spot and was getting paid $46,000 a year right out of the gate. This felt like I won an award. To be twenty-three years old and making that amount as a single woman made me feel successful. I was working at two schools in New Britain at the time and looked forward to teaching the students to the best of my ability. I taught middle school strings. This took up most of my time because I discovered there was no curriculum. The string teachers and I had to come up with the curriculum on our own.

What I also quickly discovered was that the students had no instruments. I called practically every music store to see if I could get the students some instruments at a discounted price. They were willing to help me. I reached out to celebrities back in 2013 to share my tweets so I could get funding for my students. A celebrity did share it and I was thankful. Some parents purchased or rented the instrument for their children, but some of them did neither. They either didn't have the funds or didn't take it seriously. I worked overtime at both schools. I would get there at 7 am before school started and leave at 6 pm when most of the teachers left. My life was school, eat dinner, sleep, and on the weekends support my students. I reached out to the music supervisor to have my students who wanted to take private lessons and potentially pursue a career in a special music program.

I was able to put together a program where I would work

with another professional violinist who brought students together in a chamber orchestra and had them play more difficult pieces. My life was devoted to my beloved students. I enjoyed the creative freedom that I thought I had in the school. However, I could tell based off how administration treated me that they didn't like my strong personality. I wasn't rude, but I was very independent and focused on getting my students to excel and be their best.

Administration didn't like change and couldn't grasp the vision that I was seeing for my students. Admittedly I didn't know everything I was doing, but I tried my best with the knowledge that I had and took time to learn what I thought I needed to learn. I taught them to the best of my ability at the time. I knew my strengths and weaknesses as a teacher. The students were learning and progressing fast.

Despite this, I felt as if I wasn't doing enough because of my horrible student teaching experience, but my teaching style worked for my students. Their intonation and bow hold improved within a week. It was impressive to see and made me happy that they were succeeding. The students were amazing, but as time went on, I started to feel drained and not supported by the administration. No one was helping me get the students their instruments and they didn't care about the music program.

I started seeing favoritism at one of the schools I went to. Some of the teachers kissed the ass of the people in administration. I wasn't one of those people and focused on my students. I got along great with the gym teacher, some music teachers at my other school, and the secretary. I wasn't there to make friends because I saw how people backstabbed each other at my previous jobs. I wanted to do my job and go home to prepare for the next day. After one month I was miserable and didn't look forward to going to work.

I was stressed and angry more so than depressed. I only looked forward to leaving school and eating. I felt as though I was stuck there because my mom had retired and if I had left there my health insurance would have been revoked. I kept saying that I didn't want to be there, and I wanted to leave. I would say this in my head and to my mom.

One day while I was teaching, a student was being disrespectful. Normally she was quiet and pleasant, but that day she was in rare form. She threatened to leave my classroom and I had blocked the door because students weren't supposed to walk out unattended.

The student pushed my arm in an upward motion and then out resulting in an injury. I reported the incident after realizing that my arm was actually hurt. When I went home it got worse and I had to go to the doctor. The doctor was a workers' compensation doctor who also worked with the school. He gave me a doctor's note that said I would be out for two weeks. The injury got progressively worse. I had swelling and numbness from the hands up to my neck.

Sometimes I would lose oxygen to my brain and had to sit down. I had to lie down and rest often. That two-week note turned into two months. I was no longer able to feed myself because I had nerve damage. I got my wish to not be in school, but it was a painful wish. I realized that I was able to manifest what I wanted but needed to specify next time. Physical therapy was fun and what I needed to feel a sense of comfort. My arm being in a sling was no fun at all. While I was out of school there were various substitute teachers who were teaching my students.

I had to leave a sub plan folder which I created ahead of time. I missed the students but hated those schools and the administration. I didn't like the vibe, the tension, or the politics. They grossed me out and didn't make me feel free. The administration was getting frustrated with me being out so long. They didn't care about my injury and wanted to replace me.

Administration contacted the doctor, and I was forced to

come back. The doctor wrote me a note that indicated I was supposed to be on light duty. When I came back the note was being disregarded and I was on full duty.

At one of the other schools the principal barely spoke to me. However, when I got back to school and immediately had to go home because I lacked oxygen, she had a lot to say. This bitch started yelling at me for being out of school with a legitimate injury.

I was fuming because she was becoming aggressive. I talked my shit and stood my ground, but I wanted to hit her. My brain immediately was thinking, "If this bitch hits me how am I going to fight her with one arm?" These people at these schools were psycho.

When I was busting my ass, the administration didn't even bother to show up at the music department to see the students play. She simply wanted me gone and they wanted to get rid of me. The next day I was at the other school, and they had me on lunch duty after teaching a regular music class.

Again, they violated what was written on the doctor's note. Once I was standing and doing lunch duty in the cafeteria. I kindly told the assistant principal that I was light-headed and had to sit down. He was two-faced and didn't like me anyways, but he was the one I had to report to if I wanted to leave lunch duty.

He said, "Okay." I went back to my class and sat down. That weekend I was over my aunt's house along with my mom. My mom and aunt are intuitive and know things. They both told me that the school was going to fire me.

Sure enough that same week I was fired. The Teacher's Union that was supposed to be backing the teachers was bullshit. At that meeting the head of the Teacher's Union was trying to get me to quit. My mom told me not to quit and said, "Let them fire you." I let them fire me and then I filed a lawsuit. A family friend referred me to a Worker's Compensation Lawyer"

He was excellent and was appalled at the behavior of the school. To my surprise the reason why I was fired was because the guy who was the assistant principal told them that I said the students in the cafeteria were noisy. He lied. When I was fired, I felt hopeless and had no direction as to what I was going to do.

CHAPTER 6

$\mathcal{A}$ woman I met at a vegan food truck told me that it was good I was fired, and she said there was something better. At the time I didn't understand that concept, but soon after I did. I sued them and won the case. I felt free and realized this was the beginning of a new journey for me. After dealing with difficult experiences back-to-back I took time out to reflect and meditate.

I decided that I was going to start living life according to my standards and my peace and recognized my peace was more important. I craved my peace no matter what that looked like. I started sleeping more and studying my sleep patterns. Reflecting on how I felt when I got up extremely early to go to school and my past jobs encouraged me to rest more.

I was adamant about not repeating the same toxic, draining cycle where I put my mental health last. I did what it took to keep me peaceful. My body needed at least 9 hours of sleep and beyond every day. It was as if it had been deprived of sleep for many years.

Running consistently every day, praying, meditating, and reading my Bible became the norm. I would go on a spiritual fast from time to time so I could get rid of things that were causing me to feel stuck on my spiritual and health journey. I would do three-day fasts and allow myself to cleanse and detox.

Physical therapy was a place I still had to go to every week. As I was going through my healing process after graduating school, being fired, and filing a lawsuit I started struggling with eating habits. I so badly wanted to lose weight to get some boy's attention and my goal was 123 lbs. I was eating a half of a banana, a handful of walnuts, and some applesauce for 4 weeks straight. My joints started hurting and I would run for most of the day until I would sweat profusely.

I met my goal and saw the boy at a gathering, but nothing came from that. I regretted not dating him years ago when I first got into the Church. At the Church I attended dating was frowned upon, so I was single and celibate since I graduated high school up until this time at age twenty-three. He wasn't interested, but mentally I had never let him go. I held onto him out of sheer guilt and regret. He didn't acknowledge my appearance when I saw him, but that was my first lesson in not losing weight for other people. Later I learned to do things solely for myself.

After a while I wanted to do something different with my life. I saw this gym on television, and it was unlike any training that I had when I went to Planet Fitness. I had taken a six-week weight-training course when I went to Central Connecticut State University and it was one of my favorite courses. When I was going through a rough time mentally training kept my mind focused on having fun. Releasing those endorphins were necessary for me and what I was dealing with at the time.

Immediately when I saw this gym on television I wanted to

join. It was a gym at West Hartford nearby my apartment at Newington, Connecticut. The day I joined I was ecstatic. I was thin, but I wanted to be more in shape. My breasts were always big, and I didn't go get a bra fitting so they felt heavy wearing the wrong-size bra. I also had a few injuries from my 2007 car accident, 2009 car accident and the recent injury in 2013, which didn't help the back pain I was experiencing.

The gym saved me from having breast reduction surgery, which I was happy about. My first day there at that gym consisted of me doing a consultation. During the consultation I learned how to foam roll and do basic foundational movements so I could move correctly and efficiently. Kettle bells instantly became my favorite. I was happy to shape my physique and to move better as well. I picked up my groceries without hurting myself. If I washed the clothes, I picked up the basket the way I would lift a barbell.

Those movements were incorporated into my everyday life to prevent injury. After the consultation I officially joined the gym the same day in 2014. I had rested for a while and got my mental health back on track. I was ready to discipline myself and make boot camp a part of my everyday routine.

Faithfully getting up to pray at 4:20 am every single day to align myself and keep my mind focused on peace was what I needed. Then I bathed, cleaned myself up, did my hair, and got to the gym every day at 7:00 am.

It was an amazing start to my day and the trainers were great. Besides my first ex-boyfriend, some best boyfriends, and a few uncles in the past I was used to abusive men. I was used to men not caring about me because the abuse that I had experienced clouded my perception of the good men I came across. The abuse was traumatic so when I went to boot camp and the male trainers there cared about me and showed concern about my injuries, I was shocked.

This allowed me to start opening up a bit more and realize

that not everyone is here to hurt me. I felt safe around the opposite sex and that meant a lot. The majority of the time I didn't feel safe or cared for nor did I think that I deserved it. When my father died, I delved heavily into my masculine energy and when men cared for me it was hard to receive. It made me feel mushy. To feel that people of the opposite sex cared about me was similar to the Grinch growing a heart.

I was grateful for this brand-new opportunity to be able to be more in my feminine energy and receive. I didn't open up fully, but this was a good start. When I wasn't at the gym, I was home figuring out what I wanted to do as a career. I contemplated being a music teacher in the school system again but was doubtful about the schools hiring me since I was fired. Blogging seemed like a viable option, so I started looking into that.

Website design was the main focus because I needed a place to blog. I reached out to a web and graphic design agency to design a website for me. My very first website was called "From The Root". The concept behind it was that in order to progress in life you had to get to the root of the problem. It was a holistic website that focused on fitness, beauty, cooking, blogs, health, and more.

My goal was to make funds as a blogger. This didn't pan out too well because I didn't know how to make funds as a blogger. I was a guest blogger on some sites and did interviews for blogs but blogging itself was a failure. I also started a YouTube channel back then, which was becoming popular. I used to talk about women's health and would focus on endometriosis and menstrual cycles.

People found those videos to be informative and I had a great time, sharing the info to help people. Eating a plant-based and vegan diet helped me reverse the disease. After eight painful years of dealing with endometriosis I had finally gotten rid of it at the age of twenty-three. I read Dr. Joel Fuhrman's *Eat To Live* book and did a holistic health protocol of my own to get rid of this debilitating disease.

Health became something I was passionate about when I saw how it helped my mom and me. By this time, she had lost 200 lbs. eating healthily without surgery and I avoided having a third laparoscopy surgery for endometriosis. My mom went to Dr. Fuhrman's Nutrition Education Institute to become a health coach and when she would study, I found myself memorizing all the health info.

She inspired me to become a health coach. I found that I had a passion for it and started searching for places that offered a holistic course. The next year I came across this holistic health coaching school at Connecticut. They offered a holistic health coach course, but before becoming certified I had to go to their retreat.

I stayed at the retreat for one week and ate all raw vegetables, drank green juices, and teas. Everyone there had to do enemas as well. I hated doing the enemas. The thought of sticking tubes up my ass every night felt like a chore.

One of my favorite moments there was when I drank hot water with lemon, cayenne, and salt. This helped me fight my cravings. Prior to me entering the holistic health school I attended I was following the 80/10/10 diet and eating 9 bananas and 60 medjool dates a day.

I was still going to the gym but took a week off to attend the retreat. I turned into a complete gym rat as well during that time. When I would leave boot camp, I went to cycling class five, sometimes six days a week. One day I had a health scare in cycling class. I got on the bike and knew I was sitting on the seat of the bike. However, I could see the floor in front of my face. I realized that I was experiencing severe dizziness and had to leave immediately. I sat down in my car for a minute before I went home to gain balance. When I got home, I was concerned about my health because I had experienced dizziness before, but not to that extent. I refused to go get tested because I was on a health nut kick and wanted to heal myself.

I was glad to go to the holistic health school shortly after. A few days into my stay I had horrible detox to the point where I felt dizzy and had to stay in my room. The staff were very kind and came to check on me. Despite this, I felt it was a great cleansing experience. I was also able to share my story with other trustworthy people. I used to look forward to relaxing in the infrared sauna and drinking my nightly teas sweetened with Stevia. The Stevia was also a big help in curbing cravings.

When it was time to go home, I didn't want to leave. I met new people who were fun, vibrant, and into health. It was great to make new connections. During this time, I was still blogging, taking violin lessons with a holistic violin teacher, and furthering my violin teaching pedagogy to be able to have my own private music studio. I wanted to learn everything that I wasn't taught in school so I could be the best teacher to those students.

I signed up for my holistic violin teacher's online academy, which taught me how to teach pre-k to adult. This is what I wish I had in school, but thankful I stumbled upon this teaching methodology. I never liked to do everything verbatim so also started to come up with my own methodology. The technique she used became the foundation of my teaching, but not the exact same way that I taught my students.

She helped me immensely with my playing and perfecting my very own technique. She also took a business and marketing class, so she was helping me market. I was so stressed working with her, and this started a horrible food addiction. My weight shot up rapidly from 127 lbs. to 146 lbs. in a matter of months.

I was eating jars of peanut butter a day, Kit's Organics bars, and an entire jar of Dr. Fuhrman's Date Nut Pop 'Ems. I was out of control and didn't know how to stop. This food addiction lasted for some time and pushed my health over the edge once I got into the holistic health coaching school. I spoke to the holistic violin teacher and let her know that I didn't want to do the marketing anymore.

Putting out my very own ad for violin teaching served me well because people started to find me and reach out to me to sign their children up for lessons. I became a traveling violin teacher. The children were so cute and were happy to play the violin. I had a blast creating their notes and laminating them. I made a musical board game from scratch that they enjoyed, and starter violins from tissue boxes.

I taught for a couple months, but my health was not the greatest so I had to notify the parents and let them know that I would no longer be teaching. The children adored me even the ones who didn't open up to any adults. Their parents loved me and gave me gifts. I was sad to leave them, but my health had to come first. By this time, I incorporated essential oils in my health routine, and this helped me boost my immune system.

The owner of the holistic health coaching school taught an essential oils class a few months back before I stayed at the retreat. I fell in love with them, and they were a huge help in getting rid of endometriosis and the herpes virus I had.

That herpes virus I had took eight years to go away. No holistic doctors were able to help me get rid of it. I had reached out to one of them thinking they would give me some tinctures or some herbs for it. Instead like any other doctor would she recommended that I take an antibiotic. I was surprised, but in order to not go blind I took heed to her recommendation. Attending the essential oils class was a lifesaver and came just in time before the herpes virus came back again. The woman teaching taught on viruses, antibiotics, cellular and intra cellular function.

The information was enlightening so I purchased the essential oils. When I started using them, I noticed that the virus never came back again. I stopped getting the flu and having problems breathing as well. I was always sick from a baby so was no stranger to health issues. This is partly why I went to school to be a health coach. I wanted to know what was wrong with my body.

As a baby I was birthed with a compromised immune system due to my mom's poor diet and my father's smoking and drinking habits. At age five I had pink eye and would contract this disease a total of thirty times throughout my life. At age seven I was diagnosed with asthma and was on prednisone and albuterol. When I was ten years old, I started my period and was getting several vaccines at the same time. When I was twelve I had strep throat and a crooked mouth for an unexplained reason.

At age fifteen I was diagnosed with Stage IV Endometriosis, the herpes virus and vertigo at sixteen years old. I was also on antibiotics, a bunch of meds, and getting more vaccines. Before I went back to the holistic health coaching school at age twenty-five to become a Certified Holistic Health Coach, I went to have blood tests done to see why I almost fell of the bike at cycling class.

To my astonishment I had liver damage and diabetes. My weight was around 157 lbs., I had fat rolls, my skin was grayish brown, and my hair wouldn't grow for three years. I didn't look like myself and struggled with my identity. I still struggled with food addiction and hated the way I looked in clothes.

I didn't get the answers that I wanted at the school and had no clue why my health was so bad at this time. I was hungry all the time and eventually found out that I was leptin resistant. The owner of the school stated that there was more than enough food and I was able to eat all I wanted. However, when I asked for more food, it was denied, which I thought was odd and unnecessary.

My blood sugar was out of whack, I paid to stay at the hotel where the in-person business portion of the online program was held and felt hungry all the time. Leaving the hotel and deciding to commute so I could feel satiated at home seemed like the better option.

When I graduated from the holistic health coaching school, I looked forward to helping people with various ailments. My certification had allowed me to help everyone who wanted to lose weight to people dealing with terminal illness. I lost some people that I loved to cancer so those were the first clients I wanted to work with. I didn't charge them because I was a new coach, and it was a serious illness. One family had agreed to work with me and then declined the help because they gave their family member up for dead. I gave someone a cancer protocol and they were able to shrink their cancerous tumor. I also taught essential oil classes to people who had cancer and/or had relatives who had cancer.

I was sick yet trying to help the sick for free, which was bringing in no income. Before I took in paying health-coaching clients I devoted my time to teaching essential oil classes and traveling. I worked for a popular essential oil company and enjoyed discovering the amazing benefits of these delicious plant extracts. I spent hours reading up on the properties of each essential oil and their chemical constituents. I became an essential oil expert and shared how amazing they were with other people. This passion for helping people moved me up in this essential oil company very fast. Within three months I hit a leadership position. This was rare, but I did it and it was a rewarding feeling.

The reward turned into an award when I received a trophy at the yearly convention. This convention took place in Utah. I was advised not to go to the convention because I was dealing with major health issues, but I went anyway. I was looking forward to receiving my award. I worked in network marketing dynamic and was placed in the down line of the woman who was the owner of the holistic health coaching school.

She stayed in the hotel room with two other people and me. She was in a leadership position already, but had some difficulties with placement, name changes, etc. The day I went to accept the award I felt as though she was jealous and bitter. Instead of coming with us to cheer me on she said, "I'm going to the gym."

There were no well wishes or anything. I was unbothered and went on stage to accept my award with those who were happy for me. It took place in front of thousands of people, and I felt an enormous amount of joy. Science day at convention was boring to the majority of the people there, but intriguing and exciting to me.

I was blown away at the intricate properties that the medical director was educating us on. These were properties you couldn't find on the company website or in a regular essential oil book. Holistic health was my focus and I wanted to know how the oils could benefit me on a mental, emotional, physical, and spiritual level.

I taught classes for one year, but my health was still not that great. People started inviting me to teach at juice bars on various occasions. I enjoyed seeing brand new faces of people wanting to learn about essential oils. Listening to their stories and hearing the results of how the oils helped them made me feel amazing.

I would always hear someone at the essential oil company

talking about how the oils were beyond organic because they were indigenous. They also discussed their spiritual properties and how certain frequencies could fight off several diseases.

This was enlightening to hear and an omen to me because during this time I was finding out my nationality, ancestry, history, and birthright. Come to find out I was indigenous and not black or African American like I was being told.

Soon I discovered that I had a rich ancestry that dated back to ancient times. My ancestors had built the ancient pyramids, schools, universities, and architecture. They were astrologers, medical doctors, scientists, philosophers, psychics, musicians, and basically everything you could think of.

I read books, such as *Nature Knows No Color-Line* by J.A. Rogers, and *The Story of the Moors in Spain* by Stanley Lane-Poole. Another book that I read was *They Came Before Columbus* by Ivan Van Sertima and *Ancient and Modern Britons Volume I and Volume II* by David Mac-Ritchie. I used to love studying the Moorish sculptures and ancient features. It was fascinating and thrilling. I had a revelation about this history because I was never taught that.

As a music lover I was elated to find out that Mozart was a Moor. He was one of my favorite composers and I resonated with his music. The way he would express himself in his pieces and without words asked the violin player to bring it to life was peaceful brilliance of artistry.

Beethoven and Haydn were also Moors. This made me feel happy because in college we were taught that Classical Music originated from people who were not Moor Americans. Everyone I saw looked nothing like me and I thought we were a talentless people. This discovery uplifted my spirits.

My nationality is Moor American from the ancient Canaanites and Moabites. Once I found out who I was I made a public declaration declaring my nationality as Moor American and denouncing myself as a color. All this information was new to me and led me down a deep rabbit hole.

I felt bamboozled by the media and the schools. I was told that I came from slaves and my ancestors were poor and stupid. These were all lies to make melanated people feel inferior and I was enraged. It took time to adjust and digest this information. Moor Americans are also considered Aboriginal Indigenous. This was shocking news to me because the way the media portrays indigenous people is light-skinned or pale.

I recall sharing to someone that I was Aboriginal Indigenous, and they were surprised as well because of my slightly darker complexion. I had many questions about Moor Americans and one of those questions were, "Why isn't anyone talking about this history?" It turns out that the Moors were everywhere and ruled the world.

It was because of this that it was a well-kept secret. There was a specific process that had to be taken to publicly declare my nationality. The reason for declaring my nationality publicly was to make it known to the so-called people running government that I am no longer a part of their system.

This process required me to obtain different identification from the majority of the population. I now have a National Identification Card and a Right To Travel Card and no longer use certain identification. On top of this I had a name correction because the Moors are identified by titles.

I also had a spiritual awakening at this time and the original name I was given, which was SHELBY RICKS was not suiting me anymore. This journey ignited the discovery of a brand-new appellation. My Spirit kept showing me an A in my third eye and shared with me a specific movie. In that movie the girl's name meant Gift from God. Creator and Spirit guided me to take on the Chaldean version, which is modern day Hebrew version of that name. My appellation is now Avishai and my title is El. Avishai is Gift from God and El means lawgiver. This name correction caused a complete uproar within my family. Many people didn't understand what was happening. They thought I left them and was being disrespectful to the matriarch of the family. They thought the Moors were an organization and I was in some sort of cult. At this time, I felt like Shaquile Sunflower on the television show *Martin*.

When I changed my appellation, I was still dealing with health issues and decided to stop taking violin lessons at this time. I couldn't even get up off the floor, so I lay on the floor to sleep. I used to pray down there a lot so when I went to sleep, I stayed down there. I used to get these visions of flowers and ancient looking graves. My Spirit prompted me to get tattoos. I thought that this would be frowned upon on the Church, but I went and got it anyways. The holistic violin teacher saw my new tattoos and got upset with me about it because I spent funds on tattoos. She also discontinued my expensive membership that I paid in full to her academy. I tried to reason with her about it and the response from her assistant was that the program was gone.

One thing I never did at this time was go against what my Spirit told me to do. After I went to get those tattoos, I started to feel better. My liver didn't hurt as much, I was walking on my own again, and I felt like a badass. Out of respect I called my aunt who was also my Pastor to let her know that I got tattoos. She didn't care and in fact she liked them. Her support made me feel better because people were saying mean things and even calling me a whore.

I was teaching Sunday School for a bit and enjoyed teaching the class. My Spirit would reveal to me various revelations from the Bible, and I loved flowing. Providing people with solutions and imparting in their lives to help them progress was a rewarding feeling.

One week before I taught Sunday School again my Bible kept flipping to a scripture in the Old Testament about artisans. Each time I opened it, it would flip back. When I taught in Sunday School again, I mentioned to everyone about starting their own businesses, growing their own food, and governing themselves. Everyone wasn't on board, so I shook the dust off of my feet, decided to stay home, and not teach anymore.

As time progressed and as my studying increased, I discovered that the Bible wasn't literal as it was being taught. There were metaphors, allegory, anthropomorphic, amongst other things. I memorized many scriptures and with this newfound information I went back over them.

I wanted to decipher them and understand them to their full capacity. Surprisingly the Bible commonly referred to as the Holy Bible, in Greek is Helios Biblios. Helios Biblios is the Book of the Sun or the Sun Book. The Sun Book refers to astrology. Astrology is considered demonic and of hell to the Church. It was seriously comical to find this out because two years ago back in 2014 I saw electrical writing on the closet door in my room. Then Spirit woke me up and said, "Follow the Morning Star." I took what Spirit said and looked up 'morning star' in my Bible. I realized that the wise men followed the stars.In doing my research I came across Exodus, which said, "...and this shall be the beginning of months..." I thought, "Wait a second isn't January the New Year? Why is Exodus telling everyone that March is the New Year?" Astrologically Aries is the beginning of months. Fast-forward two years later to 2016 and everything started to make sense.

I tried to talk about this in Church but was shut down. Everyone has beliefs and I respect that. However, since I was on a different path, I didn't see the reason for me to attend Church anymore. Actually, I kept trying to step foot in the Church and my body got physically nauseas. I would tell my mom this and say, "It's the weirdest thing. I keep getting nauseas."

My aunt and pastor were truly instrumental in igniting my spiritual gifts and imparting wisdom, knowledge, and understanding in my life. She was there for me at several low points, and I will always be grateful for that and still love her. I let her and other church members know how I felt and why I didn't feel like coming to Church.

Shortly after I left and started on a spiritual journey. I added metaphysical books to my Bible reads and studied etymology as well. Astrology became a new passion as well and I started talking about it all the time. I found it to be crucial in discovering who I was. People were upset that I was gone and felt betrayed. They thought I was demonic and governed by Satan. My life looked like it was taking a turn for the worse at this point. My business was failing because I didn't have identification they recognized. I lost hundreds of customers in a business that should have thrived. My lights got shut off as did the electricity. It was cold and thankfully someone who I will always appreciate, and is one of the most loyal people I know, helped get my lights turned back on. Within one month I wasn't able to pay the rent and was losing everything.

The policy enforcers known as police by the majority of people were also following me as I was in my car. One day two of them stopped me again and threatened to have me arrested if I didn't provide them with identification that I no longer had as an Aboriginal Indigenous person. I stood my ground and cussed out the aggressive policy enforcer. He started pulling at his bootstrap where his gun and taser were. He also started stuttering because I knew my rights.

After this verbal altercation I was left with a ticket and told that there would be a warrant out for my arrest. I contacted the proper people in position and the case was thrown out. It pays to know law and command your freedom to be so...so may it be. No one was with me when I had to stand up for myself against two policy enforcers. However, I had my mom on the phone as a witness just in case something went haywire.

I was still living with my mom due to the fact that I couldn't work a regular job because I was sick the whole time, couldn't work, and needed assistance. I was homeless after and not living on the street. My uncle offered my mom and I a chance to stay with him and my cousin.

I didn't want to move in with anybody. Although I lost everything and didn't have funds, I was going to stay in my car and think of a hustle that would bring me financial stability. My mom encouraged me to move in and I did so reluctantly. I was appreciative that he offered to let us stay there. A bunch of emotions were running through me at this time. I was pissed at a lot of people for turning their backs on me and no one was willing to put any of my belongings in storage or in their base-ment. Everyone my mom and I asked told me, "No" and they had no remorse. No one cared so I became full of fucking rage. I started cutting people off one by one the way Bilie Eilish sang it in *You Should See Me in a Crown*.

My mom and I couldn't fit everything in my uncle's place, so we put everything in storage. Unfortunately, we weren't able to afford for them to keep our belongings in storage, so they threw or stuff away. I had music books in storage, sentimental things packed away, and other things that I wanted to keep. I resented my mom because I didn't want my stuff in storage and storage thought everything was hers. I told her to call them and see if they could waive the fee or give her an extension. They gave her an extension and then sold the storage unit. My mom couldn't keep up with the payments and refused to call her again to get an extension. All my stuff was completely gone. I cried about this off and on for the duration of my stay at my uncle's house. It hurt me to the core that all my memories and accomplishments were in the fucking trash somewhere. My mom felt bad, and I was pissed at her.

I told her that she thinks too much within a box and not outside the box. I told her that they would have worked with her, but she had limited thinking. I was outraged, but as time went on, I forgave her because she didn't do it intentionally.

After losing everything in storage the car broke down. Moving in with relatives was a major adjustment. Having a car lightened the load because I was away from home all day. Losing the car was a huge disappointment. I now had to take public transportation from Hartford, where my relatives stayed, to wherever I needed to go during the day. The area was terrible. There were homeless people in that area, which made me feel grateful I had a bed to lie in. However, my mom and I had to stay in the same bed, and I wasn't comfortable in that bed. Nothing felt like it belonged to me. The entire time I was there I felt out of place. As someone who is hypersensitive to the energies around them, I constantly felt as if my Spirit wanted to be somewhere else, but my fleshly body was stuck.

I made the most out of each day and took public transportation to Whole Foods and the gym. Those places made me feel some sense of normalcy because I used to frequent similar places when we stayed at the apartment at Newington. Going to the buffet at Whole Foods in the summer and sitting outside in the gorgeous weather while enjoying delicious food was relaxing.

I used to record videos on social media to show my food and encourage people to eat more plant-based or vegan. I joined a gym in Newington, a private club with not too people there. I loved going into the various rooms they had for different exer-cises. The med balls, the barbells, and dumbbells were my favorite. It was great to release endorphins dealing with all the stress of losing everything that you had. Where I got dropped off at this gym was dangerous. A car could have hit me at any given time. It was hard to cross the street because it was a high-way. This street was not too far from where my old hairdresser used to live. She did my hair for four years, but once I declared my nationality she started to change. I stopped getting a perm back in 2013 when I started going to her organic salon and my hair was naturally curly. Perms almost made me go bald. I was getting them from the time I was five years old up until twenty-three-years- old.

CHAPTER 7

*D*oing my naturally curly hair didn't used to be a problem for my most recent hairdresser. However, times change, and she flipped. Eventually she got tired of doing it and was encouraging me to get a keratin treatment that was expensive for me at the time and something I was allergic to. It was either I had to get that or me not go to her.

I decided not to go to her anymore and I was without a hairdresser for about a year. Public transportation wasn't bad at first, but then I started getting sexually harassed by people on the bus. Some of the men would get close to me and stare at me. Other men would try to kidnap me, and one threatened to take me to his home.

I remember one incident on the bus where this drunk guy was yelling at me, standing in in close proximity. He called me a bitch and said mean things. I was quiet because I was waiting to knock his ass out. Someone beat me to the punch and pushed him off the bus. I was grateful to that man for standing up for me.

.   .   .

I told some male relatives what was happening, but they didn't say or do anything about it. One relative asked me, "What did you do for people to be aggressive towards you?" The behaviors of most people who were family or non-related were mind blowing to me.

Most people didn't show compassion or empathy. They were concerned with themselves and their lives. I got used to cutting people off and not speaking to them. This made me more detached as a person than I ever was. It was nothing to let go of people and go on about my life. I didn't miss them, didn't want to speak with them, and started setting strict boundaries about what I was going to tolerate and not tolerate anymore.

The harassment got increasingly worse. I stopped going to the gym where it was hard to cross the street and decided to switch gyms. One night a male bus driver went off route and stopped in a dark, secluded parking lot. I kept asking him where he was going, and he wasn't answering me. I wore my hair straight in a ponytail with the back out, some black leggings, and a black North Face jacket. My phone was dead at this time, but I faked like I was calling someone on the phone to report him. He freaked out and got nervous. Then he brought me to the gym.

When I was getting off the bus he said, "Did you call some-one?" I gave him no response. When I walked inside the gym, I felt safe, but uneasy. This could have gone badly if I hadn't thought quickly on my feet. Who knew what he would have done? The experience was traumatic; I made sure to charge my phone in the gym.

Once I got home my mom was upset about this incident. I reported it to the bus company, but no one did anything. The man still drove the bus, but I didn't get on with him because I didn't feel safe. One of my cousins showed concern when she spoke to my mom on the phone and told me to call the policy enforcers. Most people say police, but as an Aboriginal Indigenous person I refer to them as policy enforcers. I didn't contact them, but my mom started taking the bus with me. I was thankful to be around her energy. As someone who is hypersensitive to energies, being around all that energy was draining. I was constantly cleansing myself and transmuting other people's energies. Sometimes I absorbed and sometimes I observed. Eventually I mastered the art of transmutation to protect my peace.

As a natural healer I was attracting broken people and energy vampires when I would ride the bus. One day as I was waiting for the bus to come this woman came up to me and started telling me her life story. I let her talk to me for about an hour. When she was done, I felt drained, but she felt better. That was the first and last time I ever let that happen. I saw her again and when I saw her coming I either had my headphones on or completely ignored her. Protecting my peace was important.

Prior to my mom getting on the bus with me I would take the bus to see my maternal grandmother on the North End of Hartford. This was a bad area, but I loved my maternal grandmother. Being around her felt peaceful, but the bus ride there was horrendous.

The bus would go pick up mental health patients who were something out of the movie *One Flew Over The Cuckoo's Nest*. Other people who were not mental health patients should have been admitted as well. There were so many angry and toxic people on that bus.

I was happy when everyone got off the bus or I was the only one. Originally my mom and I were going to stay with my maternal grandmother, but there was conflict because family members visited her. They didn't like the fact that I declared my nationality at the time, nor did they understand it. To keep the peace, we stayed with my uncle and cousin.

From time to time my mom and I spent the night over my maternal grandmother's house. One night I was going back to my uncle's house. The buses stopped running and I thought they ran all night, so I was without transportation. I didn't want to bother any family members who had children, so I called people who I still spoke to who didn't have children.

They didn't want to come pick me up. There was no remorse in their responses, but there was a complete change in how I dealt with them, which was not at all. My maternal grandmother already had breathing issues and heart problems. She was worried and I hated that she was worried about me not getting home.

In fact, I went over there that day to help my mom take care of her. She wanted to call people to get me, but I told her that I would walk back home. That night I walked from the North End around 11:00 pm EST to downtown. You literally had to be a psycho to walk that long ass distance late at night. Anything could have happened, and the area was terrible.

Random men were pulling up trying to talk to me. I refused and kept walking. In all honesty I had fun walking out late at night. When I was walking, I said, "I'm going to bring my own vibe." After I said this, I created a force field around me to shield me from lower vibrational frequencies and I felt free.

I was even tempted to walk into a party they were having on Albany Avenue. This reminded me of my free nature I had back in high school. I didn't care what I was doing and whom I was with as long as I was having fun. I skipped the party and made sure I got home.

Before I got home, I made a pit stop at CVS. A girl walked in without her wig and bloody. She immediately came to me and said, "I was jumped by twelve people," near Garden Street and another street she had mentioned.

I felt so bad for her, but her and her boyfriend fought back. She was still walking and coherent. Thankfully that wasn't me because I was literally near that area and boldly walked with my big brown vegan leather handbag.

When I got home, I called my mom to let her know that I got home safely. I made sure to leave my maternal grandmother's house early next time to avoid having to walk home again. My mom was my guardian angel to take the bus with me. It kept people from randomly talking to me and being verbally abusive.

Prior to her deciding to come with me I was dealing with aggressive passengers and bus drivers. I never put up with anybody's shit. I got in a bus driver's face before because she was being rude and condescending to me for no reason. I cussed out another man for urinating outside in public before getting on the bus. I was so enraged because children could have seen that. He shut his mouth and left me alone. Another man cut me in line and gave me an attitude because he didn't want to wait to get on the bus like everybody else. I blacked out and went off. All I remember was a tall, grown man looking like a scared little boy when I was finished with him. I got into it with so many people for being myself. I never provoked anybody and minded my own business, but no one was going to disrespect me. I almost got into it with a girl that was on the bus at the North End of Hartford, but she evaded my question. I was ready to punch her. Thankfully that didn't happen. I was ready to fight anybody and everybody every time I got on the bus. The energy was low vibrational. I hated taking the bus by myself in the winter. It was cold and I would be out from early in the after-noon until nighttime to get my mom and I something to eat. I had to be extremely creative and resourceful in obtaining food.

One of those ways was to sell all my jewelry and instruments to the pawnshop. This was difficult for me to do. Again, I had to part ways with my personal possessions and sentimental items so I could survive. One of the people who worked at the pawn-shop paid for me to get something to eat a few times out of the kindness of his heart. I'll forever be grateful to that man who cared about me. I saw how people were during this time. I was definitely in my feels and felt as though people wanted me to fail and strangers were showing mercy. This was and is my truth based off the actions of other people.

I was eating a lot of processed foods, which was a change from the smoothies I was drinking and salads I was eating at Newington. This situation sent my stress levels through the roof. I was craving comfort foods that were toxic to my body and my mental health was all over the place.

I constantly felt nervous and felt like I was going to starve to death. I ate cupcakes, pizza, cookies, and kept eating the buffet. I thought I was going to be able to save all this food. My mind was constantly thinking, "How can I save this food for at least two weeks?" At this time my mom's check came in from her retirement and she paid my uncle from some of it because we stayed there. However, what was left wasn't enough for both of us.

There were no funds coming in from my end because I was extremely sickly and was being discriminated against by potential jobs for my nationality. I badly wanted to work but couldn't so I was creative and worked with what I could do from home. I gradually developed my organic, vegan, and cruelty free skincare line.

It was difficult to find a skincare brand that I wasn't allergic to. Wanting to help other people who were dealing with skin problems from liver damage and diabetes was something I was passionate about. At this time, I was wearing full coverage makeup to cover up my blemishes. I was also using about three filters on Instagram so I could look presentable and like a beautiful person.

Before I started my skincare line and launched it, I took the information that I received from my holistic health coaching and furthered my medical research studies. I began studying more on skincare and how to develop a holistic and healthy skincare line. The research on it was endless and there were so many directions I was able to go with it. It went beyond face creams, moisturizers, and facemasks.

I saw a significant correlation between nutrition and how it greatly impacted the skin on an intracellular level. The information that I was consuming on this topic gave me the mental stimulation that I needed. I thoroughly enjoyed the plethora of information on skincare and the deliciously yummy connection between skin and nutrition.

As a holistic health coach this made me feel overjoyed that everything is connected. I felt comfortable starting this skincare business. Skincare was an inexpensive business to invest in. My mom gave me some funds to start it, which I was grateful for. She saw how excited I was about it and knew I was serious. I invested the funds I was given into the ingredients for the skincare, labels, and jars. The labels were the most expensive items, and they took forever to be made. I made everything from scratch and used edible organic, vegan, and cruelty free ingredients.

Moisturizers, facial scrubs, and face creams were what my product line consisted of under Avi, which is Avishai, but shorter. People loved the products and saw immediate results with their acne, varicose veins, and even mental health. I used specific ingredients that supported overall health. The prices were affordable, and they became a hit with people.

I decided to get my skincare line noticed by the public, so I reached out to Artists & Fleas to sell my products. When I sent my application in, I was contacted by one of the managers who loved the branding of the products and wanted me to set up a table there. She also agreed to purchase one of my items, but she didn't. I called her out on it and educated her on how Universal

Law worked. She didn't respond to that, nor did I think she would.

Before I traveled from Connecticut to New York to go to Artists & Fleas I was busting my ass. I was grateful to a family member for paying for me to have a table there. I paid them right back. All of my products were handmade. I didn't use a blender or any machine to stir and mix any of my creams. I made fifty jars to take with me to New York. My mom helped me make them and label them as well. If she didn't, I would have been in trouble.

I was still sick, and it took a lot of energy to do this so I was thankful for her. I got no sleep until I got on the bus to go to Artists & Fleas. My luggage to bring the items was huge. When I arrived, I got off the bus to go on the train to get there. I took turns taking trains and taxis to arrive to and from my destination.

Working there and selling my products for two days straight was a blast. At the time I was feeling down about my living situation and all the negativity that was surrounding me. I kept hearing of people I knew gossiping about me. I almost didn't feel worthy to be there at Artists & Fleas. I felt as if I didn't fit in.

People there were kind, and we purchased each other's items. They saw me as one of them and didn't look down on me. I was there each day from 11 am – 8 pm selling my products. When it was 8 pm I went out and enjoyed myself. Treating myself felt like the right thing to do after busting my ass for two days straight.

I went to an amazing vegan restaurant called Sacred Chow on Sullivan Street at New York. The food was outstanding. There was one woman working there and the service came at rapid speed. I was shocked that one woman working by herself could bring the food out so quickly.

Everything I ate was something I normally wouldn't have eaten because of allergies, but in New York I wanted to go all out and celebrate. Around this time, I weighed 138 lbs. and was proud of myself for kicking my food addiction, going to the gym faithfully every day and sometimes twice a day. This was a huge accomplishment.

I was feeling better about my body and looked fit. When I was at Sacred Chow, I remember eating a meatball grinder and a large salad with a lot of seitan. Seitan is a vegan alternative for animal flesh and is created with vital wheat gluten. I knew I was allergic but ate it anyways because the description of the food item sounded good. It also looked good in my salad bowl.

Once I got back from New York I noticed that I was walking a little funny, my skin was oily, and my face was puffy. The first place I went to was over to my maternal grandmother's house. She had a scale in her bathroom. When I weighed myself to my astonishment, I weighed in at 149 lbs.

"Is her scale broken?" I thought to myself. "This can't be right," I said, in denial. After weighing myself multiple times and seeing the same number I finally accepted that I had gained 11 lbs. in two days. I was in complete disbelief and felt as though my efforts towards working on my body on a mental, emotional, physical, and spiritual level were forever ruined. My mom recommended a specific protocol to get the weight off and in three days I was back to normal.

I felt relief and for a short while I learned my lesson. My diet was pretty consistent at this point. I would eat fruits, veggie burgers, and veggies every day. It took some time to get there because of the stress and trauma I was dealing with, but I was determined to drop the pounds. I was 138 lbs. in New York after being 150 lbs. for the longest time. When I did my research and saw what diet worked for me this is when I lost 12 lbs. in two weeks. I realized that I didn't have to deprive myself of my favorite foods I simply needed to make them healthier. The more nutrient dense the better my body responded to it. There was no need to restrict.

Restricting foods is what sabotaged my efforts every time and made eating seem like a chore. When I discovered this method, which is now called my Eat Stress Away Method I shared it with my holistic health-coaching clients. By this time in 2018 I had one client who wanted to work on some ailments and eat healthy on a consistent basis.

I enjoyed working with ambitious and determined clients because they put the work in. These kinds of clients didn't drain me. It was encouraging to hear that this client also got rid of gallbladder disease working with me. I was coaching and selling my skincare. Always wanting to move out of my family member's house was the goal.

I couldn't move fast enough and wasn't getting enough clients. I didn't know how to market, I was sick, and felt defeated in the financial department. Shortly after working with this client my own health took a turn for the absolute worst. I remember going to the gym and going to get a smoothie afterwards. I specifically told the manager to make me a smoothie with blueberries, charcoal, and water. I was a diabetic, so I didn't want anything sweet in my smoothie. I was given a: blueberries, charcoal, banana, water, and agave syrup smoothie. When I went to catch the bus, I started to feel dizzy. When I got home, I lost my peripheral vision and a car barely missed me as I walked across the street. I told my mom what happened, and she was mad about it.

As the day went on my symptoms grew worse. I had to lie down because I was dizzy. When the next day came, I had a bad headache. Back in 2016 when I briefly attended an all women's gym, I had symptoms similar to a stroke. These felt like the same symptoms. That day I told my mom that these symptoms felt like when I thought I was having a stroke years back. She remembered this, but she wasn't in a good mood that day for whatever reason. She had an attitude with me, and I told her, "Mom I have a headache and I feel it's getting worse." She yelled at me that day and I didn't know why. I don't know what was going on with her, but shortly after my mouth looked crooked.

It was stuck like that, and this is exactly what I experienced years before. I refused to go to the hospital. As the days went on I was drooling, not speaking well and it was hard to decipher my words. After that I was partially paralyzed. A cousin of mine reached out to me and asked if I wanted to go to the hospital. As I lay down with my mouth crooked and drooling, I replied, "Yes." I was taken to the hospital and my other cousin got off work to meet my mom, another cousin, and I there. I was admitted for two days and told that I had Familial Hemiplegic Migraine with Ataxia and had to go to Physical Therapy.

I had several tests done and they thought at the time that I had multiple sclerosis as well. I was unable to afford physical therapy but was willing to go to the gym and do my own. However, I asked some of my family members to take me and they didn't. I was too sick to confront everyone involved so I didn't deal with them.

I stayed home in my bed with horrible migraines and paralysis from September to October 2018. Then I went back to the gym for a short while and took the bus to get there. My mouth was crooked, and my neck was protruding. You could visibly see that something was wrong with me. An aggressive man got on the bus and sat near me.

He told me, "Smile, life isn't that bad.

I told him, "My face is paralyzed."

He became aggressive because I wasn't making him happy and called me a black bitch and nappy headed. Prior to him saying this he couldn't stop staring at me. He had a hurt ego. I told the bus driver, and he did nothing. I couldn't defend myself because I just got out of the hospital. Everyone watched and no one intervened except for an old man with a cane and breathing issues. He was so kind, and I felt bad that he and I were exposed to that dumb, fucking idiot. I was glad when he got off the bus. I had to take a break from the gym because I was paralyzed again until December around Christmas time. This impaired my entire life. Soon I would find out that these were symptoms of a greater issue. The year 2017 would play a n important role in these symptoms.

I remember going to the gym every day that year and hurting my left shoulder and upper back. My maternal grandmother noticed that one shoulder was out of place. I also saw bruising on my chest and was sweating as I was sleeping. It took several months to get rid of what I initially thought was an injury.

Once I got better or so I thought I started training myself. A popular trainer that I followed for a few years on social media before I invested in his program had stolen from me. He didn't train me and ignored me as a client. I decided to transmute his negative, wicked actions into a positive. I took the tools that I gained from Central Connecticut State University's fitness department in 2010 and brushed up on my training skills.

This prompted me to create my own fitness programs that was getting clients to reshape their bodies in one week or less. Due to the fact that I was now paralyzed and couldn't afford physical therapy I also took my training skills and created a program for people with neurological disorders. My techniques were unheard of and unorthodox, but they worked. With Ataxia your balance is off and there's a lack of coordination. With Familial Hemiplegic Migraine there is hemiparesis, migraines, weakness, stiffness of joints, nausea, and so much more. I only did these exercises when I felt a glimpse of strength, but for the most part I was bed-ridden. About one month later I was able to walk a bit better, but still needed assistance from my mom.

I had severe PTSD where everything was hitting me like a ton of fucking bricks. I started to feel defeated and as if no one cared about my wellbeing. All the memories of the sexual harassment I had experienced made me feel violated and as if my body wasn't my own. I was also still healing from past trauma and being violated at a young age.

Feeling powerful was not in sight and it made me bitter. I didn't feel protected by the angels, the Creator, Spirit, no one. This led me down a dark path where I wanted to die. My health was shitty, I felt like a bum, some of my family didn't like me, I was constantly fighting men and women, and it was a financial struggle on a daily basis.

Toxic foods became my best friend. It was the only thing that made me happy. I ate whatever I wanted whenever I wanted as long as it was vegan. Food labels? What were those? I disregarded all the knowledge that I obtained in school when I went for health coaching.

Therapy was out of the question because I couldn't afford it. At this time, I kept getting visions of the foods that I was supposed to be eating and I knew it. I felt as though I was going backwards in time and lost any feeling of spirituality.

The path I was going down felt like the wrong path, but I was ready to give up, so I didn't care. I also knew that I was being warned and warning came before destruction, but I cared a little bit too late. In February of the New Fiscal Year 2019 two men came to my family member's apartment to paint. When they started painting my eyes started itching. The itching turned to pain and the pain turned to swelling. I was for sure that this came from my makeup because there was caffeine in it. Unbeknownst to me the paint consisted of latex and benzene a known carcinogen. I thought I simply had an allergic reaction to the paint. The next day came and my eyes were swollen shut.

I felt like I was burning, itching, and in pain all at the same time. I went into anaphylactic shock and had to be taken to the hospital. I was given allergy meds and sent back home. My body was still reacting to the fumes from the paint. I was miserable and couldn't sleep for several days. It was a nightmare. Moving out of my family member's house temporarily seemed like the only option.

My Uncle sent out a text to see who was going to take me in because I was going to die if I stayed there. No one responded. One of my cousins didn't get the message, but she called and asked how I was doing. She also offered for me to stay there. One of my aunts offered and I ended up staying with her for a couple days.

Out of many people who were sent the text I concluded only two people showed concern. I was going to literally die, and no one cared. One person even said, "I can't do it." They didn't wish me well or anything. This fueled me to get better. I started to see these scaly patches on my face and as a medical researcher and holistic health coach I studied what this might be.

It turns out I was dealing with mast cell activation disorder, which wasn't common. It was a rare disease where the body attacks itself, is allergic to pretty much everything, and you get random breakouts because of it. I felt like I was getting to the bottom of my ailments. However, when I read all of the symptoms of mast cell activation disorder, I saw that I had way more symptoms than was listed.

In that similar article that I was reading I saw mastocytosis. This disease occurs when there are an immense amount of mast cells accumulating in the skin and/or internal organs such as the liver, spleen, bone marrow, and small intestines. The mast cells protect the body from infection and releasing chemicals to create an inflammatory response. When these cells grow at abnormal rates they cause bumps on the skin, gastrointestinal issues, bone pain, and so much more.

As the list of symptoms went on there was bruising, night sweats, fever, paralysis, and the list went on. These symptoms were all symptoms that I had and were indicative of mastocytosis type IV, which was Mast Cell Leukemia. I was taken aback by this shocking information. Once I read about the symptoms, I looked at my blood tests, and my blood levels were off.

I was also taken aback by the fact that I burned from the inside out. My face looked like the people on the pig faces episode on *Twilight Zone*. I was unrecognizable and had thick layers of skin on top of each other. I could barely open my mouth to eat anything. My skin shed everywhere and was absolutely gross. I was severely traumatized by this experience and had severe PTSD. At this time, I had no doctor who could diagnose me with leukemia or cancer because I was low on funds. My body was allergic to all fruit and I was only able to eat veggies, some cashews, cheese, and corn tortillas. Shortly after my body became allergic to the corn tortillas.

I was still taking the allergy meds from the hospital, but one of the meds which were an antihistamine put me in anaphylactic shock again. I was rushed back to the hospital before I stopped breathing. They stupidly diagnosed me with dermatitis and made light of my now disfigured face.

I was infuriated with how nonchalant the people at the hospital at Hartford were. They didn't give a damn about me. The testing that they should have done based off my symptoms wasn't carried out. It took several months for my face to recover, but in March I started to see some progress.

My hair wasn't being done for a couple months due to these ailments, but in March I went back to get it done. The hairdresser I went to was located at New York. I started going to her in the winter of 2017 and stopped going to her in the summer of 2019. She was unstable and I didn't know what person I was going to get each time. I kept bumping heads with her, and she deemed me as combative because I didn't put up with her shit.

During that time when I was still going to the salon, I struggled with walking. My mom didn't want me to go. I felt weak when I walked but needed to get out of the house, so my solution was to take taxis everywhere and find places within short, walking distance. A special moment occurred when I went to Tribeca, New York and saw the *US* movie by Jordan Peele. I was going to stay home, but my Spirit kept pulling on me to go see this movie.

When I saw it I immediately knew why? The main character had her life stolen from her at a young age and at the end of the movie she took it back. I could relate to this because I felt as though my life of not having to worry about finances was taken from me. Losing everything and people bashing me made me feel like I was losing in life. I felt like a peasant in comparison with other people, but little by little I was getting my life back. I was now able to pay for my hair and some of my food. I was also progressively getting better.

The entire day I was there I kept seeing 11:11 and knew it was a sign, but from my natural eyes I saw that nothing came from it. However, I realized later on that it was an energy exchange. When I came back home from New York in March 2019 I was once again paralyzed, and bed ridden. About one month later I was told that my maternal grandmother was in the hospital for congestive heart failure.

This woman had called my mom and I every single day and I enjoyed speaking with her. She was like my older friend who had similar experiences. As a matter of fact, we had telepathic sickness. When my mom would stay with her, she would say, "Ganny experienced the same thing at the same time." It was odd, but not unusual due to me being a spiritual person.

I would check on her over the phone throughout the week

every week because I couldn't physically be over there to help her. This made me very sad and angry that I wasn't physically well to be able to help my mom take care of her. At this time, she was struggling with so many ailments that she didn't deserve. It made me feel really bad and a bit guilty, but I couldn't walk properly and was very weak so could do little to help her.

My bones would ache to the point where I would scream. When I would walk it would feel like those metal chains on Forest Gump's legs and as if my legs were breaking. However, I still wanted to be there for her because she was there for me and came to visit me during this time. I had no doubt that she would leave the hospital. Everyone looked sad, but I wasn't because she was strong, and this wasn't the only time I visited her at the hospital.

I remember three years ago when she went in for the same thing. I was in the waiting room with her and ended up yelling at the workers there for having her wait long. She was taken upstairs to her room, and they tried to give her coffee. It was declined because it was not conducive to her heart condition. Those doctors were not educated at all. She came home and my mom and I put her on a strict diet and did some herbal and plant medicine protocols. She started to feel better and lived until three years later.

I pushed myself to go and visit her that year. I remember my voice sounding just like the main character in the *US* movie. I had a lump on my chest and pain in my lungs. It took me fifteen minutes to drink an 8 oz. glass of water and hurt very badly to swallow water.

It wasn't too long before I went to see my maternal grandmother at the hospital that I was going to admit myself to the hospital. I had a death scare and couldn't get, but one breath out. My mom stayed up to make sure I woke up. I told her that she should buy me my casket because I wasn't going to make it. My mom assured me that I would make it. When I walked into my maternal grandmother room to see her, I sat down, but then I started coughing. She said, "Are you okay?" This woman was so sick and asked me how I was doing.

I left the room so she wouldn't worry. There was no doubt in my mind that I would see her again, but that was the last time I would see her. Shortly after that visit she passed away. No one including myself took this well. It was weird that she passed away, but at least she wasn't in any more pain. There was no more worries or suffering only enjoyment in the Spirit plane. On the day of her funeral, I read a poem called *Flying Free/Spirit Plane*. It was such a beautiful poem that everyone loved.

I took her death hard and collapsed to the floor after I read my poem. Most people who were at the funeral to my knowledge had no clue my legs were so bad and I had trouble walking. Yes, her death was hard, and I couldn't take the pain I felt of losing her, but my legs gave out due to my illnesses when I was walking back to my seat. I wasn't used to standing for a long period of time or walking up and down the stairs.

Although I didn't feel well, I would have never missed her funeral. She was an extraordinary person who brought me peace and love. I looked forward to going over her house every chance I got. We would eat, laugh, and enjoy ourselves. She loved to laugh. One of her favorite shows was *Downton Abbey* a British drama series. I used to laugh every time I saw her watching that show. I thought it was the cutest thing. She also liked a few more shows that I'll laughingly take to the grave. We had the same taste in one of them.

She was a free spirit and taught me valuable lessons. After her passing, funeral, and burial I reflected on all the lessons my maternal grandmother left me with. She would do what made her feel peaceful and put herself first before she took care of others. She was kindhearted and peaceful. When she had something to say that was authentic to her soul she didn't feel bad after expressing herself. These were some takeaways that I locked away in the treasures of my heart.

I will always remember and love this amazing woman, my maternal grandmother and friend. Until we meet again. Life didn't feel the same when she was gone. It felt like someone was missing and I started to feel depressed. Going on about my day was hard and when I saw people not crying, I didn't know how they did it.

From time to time I reflected on how my younger years were with her as she watched me. My mom and I used to visit her frequently at Manchester, Connecticut. I When I was around 7seven years old, I would ride my bike out there. I loved that bike, but one day I was riding down the hill and the brakes stopped working.

My bike flipped, I fell to the ground, and hurt my knee. All I could see was blood coming from my knee. My maternal grandmother was a caretaker as a career, and it didn't stop when she was at home. she and my mom cleaned up my knee and made sure I was okay.

This meant a lot because she showed me that she cared. There were some fun times at her old house. I'll never forget this boy who would always eat a bowl of blue cheese. He was a bit out there and not one to have many friends, but I adored him because he was different. He was always himself and I loved it. No one was allowed to treat him poorly while I was around. I didn't tolerate it.

CHAPTER 8

Those days were filled with great memories. I'll cherish them forever. About one month later after her passing I decided to start a podcast. I started the podcast in May 2019. At first the name of the podcast was Unfiltered Wellness, but then I changed it to Avi Unfiltered. I was going through a lot at this time and created it as an outlet.

I wanted to create a holistic health and wellness podcast that wasn't only limited to nutrition. I wanted to talk about lifestyle and the mental, emotional, physical, and spiritual aspects. My goal for this show was to have a relatable weekly conversation that would bring a sigh of relief to the listeners. I wanted them to be understood and feel a sense of community. It was rewarding to provide the community with a podcast that would make them be welcomed.

Before officially launching the podcast in June I studied what it would take to have a successful podcast. I did research on the equipment needed for each of my episodes that I would be premiering on a weekly basis. This was exciting to see all my equipment coming in. Back at Central Connecticut State University I had to use certain technological programs for music, so I was familiar with the platforms used for podcasting.

I enjoyed coming up with various topics on a weekly basis. It was a great way to express myself and walk people through life by sharing my personal experiences, providing people with the tips they needed to be successful in life, and giving messages from Spirit. Avi Unfiltered Podcast started becoming increasingly popular after having celebrity doctors on there.

Before having doctors on my show someone from a public relations company reached out to me to ask me to have their guests on the show. This was all new to me and I had no clue that my voice was going to impact so many people. About three years ago I was a holistic health and wellness guest on QUTE radio at Hartford. I spoke about the importance of essential oils and their array of health benefits.

After I did that show I thought, "I could talk on the radio all day." The day I launched my podcast I felt overjoyed because I remembered this day that I premiered on the radio. It was fun and an exciting segment to do on their show.

Speaking has been a passion of mine for some time now and it's an honor to do what I do on a weekly basis. I started the podcast at my family member's house, partially paralyzed off and on, with memory loss, and undiagnosed cancer. I was amazed at what I was able to accomplish in a year of being a host of this podcast.

My podcast was globally on the charts, Top 25 in India, Top 200 in Ghana, and Top 200 in Canada. I produced an unscripted holistic health and wellness show all by myself. This made me feel uplifted and motivated me to provide my listeners with helpful and useful information even the more.

After having Dr. Joel Fuhrman on the podcast as a guest I got to speak with him about my symptoms and told him that I had cancer. He put me on the anti-cancer diet and recommended some supplements of his. This helped me immensely and gave me more energy. The pain had lessened as well.

I still had trouble walking until I got a hold of an herbalist. This herbalist gave me a cannabis strain that revolutionized my life. I couldn't believe it when I was able to walk outside on my own again. One dose of this helped me to walk again. My legs felt like rubber. It was similar to that scene of Michael Jackson on *The Wiz* when he kept falling while walking.

It felt incredibly weird to walk again, but I did, and it felt great. I cried tears of joy and was grateful to have people like that in my life. As time went on, I was able to walk more consistently, but I was in a lot of pain. My joints were in pain, my organs were inflamed and hurting, I was bruising everywhere, and still had night sweats.

I was going back and forth to have my blood tests taken. Blood tests weren't cheap. I was at my lowest point. I was disappointed in so many people who claimed to love me and went back on their word. No one thought I was worth an explanation. I dealt with heavy depression a lot staying at my uncle's house.

Between being sick, my maternal grandmother passing away, my near death experiences, the sexual harassment, the aftermath of my face healing, the bashing that came from some fake ass people in general, and me being locked away in that room because no one offered transportation, and I couldn't walk, I was suicidal.

A few times I contemplated suicide. The first time I reached out to a family member who helped me through it. The second time I self-harmed with a butcher knife but didn't follow through with slitting my wrists. My mom cried for me when she saw me like this. I cut my hair shorter with kitchen scissors as well. I felt like I was going to explode, being locked up in that room and felt as though no one, but my mom and a small amount of family members cared.

Hardly anybody offered to come get me, come see me, or anything. I was appreciative of those who did and people who bought me groceries when I couldn't. I was thankful for that, but disappointed in people's actions. I couldn't even talk to people about being depressed without being reprimanded. The energies of these people were weird as hell.

My mom was solid during all of this, and I can't thank her enough. Tensions arose between her and I at times because we were both dealing with so much. I regretted some of my actions and so did she. Some arguments became volatile. My mom and I had our bad moments, but it got really bad at various points on our journey together. People make mistakes and I would never come off to the world as a vanilla daisy who never did bad shit.

However, I will never dim my light and hold onto guilt for all eternity for anything I've ever done. That's not healthy. She was instrumental in uplifting my spirits and if she wasn't there for me I don't know what I would have done. People literally left me for dead, but she never turned her back on me.

. . .

I had to work very hard to heal my mental health issues that occurred not only from these situations but occurred throughout my life. I would have flashbacks of trauma and then the most recent traumas would hit me. Sometimes all I could do was nothing but take some Cannabis in a smoothie or tea and go to sleep. We, as people, have an endocannabinoid system so I gave my body what it needed so I could feel a sense of balance once again.

At my lowest point people online were jealous of me left and right. People didn't see my struggles. They saw my beauty and talent. At this moment in life, I took the longest break from my podcast and social media. I had to be taken on an emergency visit to a holistic doctor's facility. My Uncle kindly drove us to New Jersey so I could be seen by one of the doctors. I had severe, life-threatening symptoms. On the ride there I felt extremely nauseas. When I got to the office, I needed my mom's assistance to walk up the stairs. I felt so dizzy and almost passed out. The doctor suspected that I had leukemia but couldn't diagnose me. He ordered several blood tests to be done so they could rule out autoimmune diseases.

This process was frustrating. All the tests kept coming back negative, except for my Ferritin Levels, which were extremely low. I hated that these tests were judged based off the Standard American tests. I did my own digging and discovered that according to optimal testing my blood levels were off. I felt like I wasn't being seen or heard by anyone at this point. You could visibly see I was sick, but the damn tests kept showing otherwise. I would wake up from my sleep and see a pool of water.

My bed was drenched with my own sweat. I had swollen lymph nodes, a cough that wouldn't go away, my face hurt, and so much more.

I was so angry that what I was going through couldn't be diagnosed. Although it was suspected that I had cancer, it couldn't be proven by those doctors. During this process I redirected my attention towards my career.

I wanted to leave my uncle's house so badly and let it be known to everyone. I was explosive and felt like a bitch at times. I was a mega bitch and irritable. I felt like spazzing the fuck out and I did on everyone in that house. I had a lot on my plate and it was too much to handle. Again, I wasn't perfect, and my mental health was horrible. I was in a different state of mind. Although I should have been focusing on resting, I wanted to focus on my stability.

I was focusing on my stability and searching for places to move. Taking action was something that I needed to do to help myself. I wasn't one to talk about it but I needed to find a place to live. At this time someone had found me through my podcast, and she immediately became a client. She stayed in Ohio and helped me find a place there.

I was ready to leave yesterday. Moving couldn't come fast enough. I was appreciative of my family member for letting my mom and I stay with him but was miserable and fed up with the living situation. I felt like my career wasn't being taken seriously. There were several times I was recording and there would be a lot of noise coming from the television or phone.

I always had to schedule in time with them to record my podcast and do other things. They were on a different path than I was, so they didn't see the significance in what I was doing.

Sometimes they would accommodate me, but it wasn't consistent. I was really trying to work even being sick and was trying to make a profit.

It was in my best interest to find a place where I could work any time I wanted, so I filled out the application to move to North Canton, Ohio. I was so excited to move there. According to my research North Canton is known to be one of the best places to stay and the safest places to stay. I felt relieved and it was a huge change from staying in a place with a high crime rate.

My client was instrumental in helping with the application process. I couldn't physically be there to sign anything, so I gave her permission to complete this process. I met with the owner via Skype, and she walked me through the process as well. Being the upfront person that I am I let it be known that I had different identification from everyone else and she was very respectful towards me, didn't discriminate, and my application was approved.

I felt as if I was getting out of prison. This was such a victory. I was glad to be on my own and free. Saying goodbye to my mom and Uncle was sad. My mom was crying, and I did feel homesick, but I refused to come back. When I arrived the apartment wasn't finished. They had just remodeled it and it looked great, but the carpeting in the living room, the kitchen, and the bathroom wasn't finished. There were also no blinds covering the windows in my room or the living room.

I despised being in an apartment with a bunch of men I didn't know who were fixing my apartment. They stayed there every day, all day, and nothing was finished. I contacted the management about this, and she took some funds off, but I didn't get a chance to relax in my own apartment.

Two days into my stay there I started coughing, itching, my nose was running excessively, and I had major trouble breathing. My bed hadn't come in yet, so I was sleeping on the floor and came into direct contact with latex and benzene once again. On top of this I was inhaling smoke and ammonia from a neighbor's apartment.

I had burned from the inside out again and I thought, "Oh no! Not this again!" I was frightened and in a panic. I thought, "This can't be possible. Just when I thought I was finally free it was happening again." I used at least three rolls of paper towel for my nose. My skin started to lump up and turn red. I could see the suppleness and elasticity from my skin quickly fade away. I contacted the management as fast as I could to talk about the negative impact the chemicals from the apartment were having on my body.

She didn't respond so I contact her again and was able to get a hold of her. She told me, "No one smokes here. I'll go and get plug ins." They installed the plug ins in the outlets, and it didn't work. This was another night I had to lay on the floor suffering. I called my mom who was very concerned, but she encouraged me to stick it out. I also wanted to stick it out and stay there because I didn't want to return to Hartford.

During this time the maintenance people were still working on my apartment. One night when I got up to use the bathroom, I noticed the toilet wasn't working. I had to call management again to let her know and she gave me a key to use the bathroom of an apartment in another building. No one occupied the apartment yet.

When I walked back to my apartment I was suffering, coughing, not able to breathe, and felt helpless. I walked back to the apartment that wasn't occupied and slept there. The next morning the maintenance people and management found me there. Instead of asking me how I was they told me I couldn't stay there. Instead of finding me another apartment while they worked on my apartment, they were gossiping about me saying that the rugs in both apartments were the same.

They heard my mouth after that because I was fed up with all of their bullshit. Management looked afraid and they were very nice after. At this time, you could visibly see something was wrong with my face. Management admitted that my face didn't look right but had no empathy or sympathy towards me. I tried to stay one more day there and I almost passed out, so I made the unfortunate decision to go back home.

I contacted management to tell her that I was leaving the apartment. She looked disappointed and a gullible person would have thought, "She's sad I'm leaving." However, she was upset that they remodeled the apartment to initially accommodate some of my allergies and now had to find another person to occupy it. That day I packed to leave her, and the maintenance manager showed up. Once again, she said, "No one smoked here." The maintenance manager told her, "Yes they do." There were even cigarettes on the ground outside.

I got out of my lease and took my heavy luggage back home.

By this time my skin started to wrinkle up like an elderly

woman and then scabbed. I had flaky patches and layers of skin on top of each other. I couldn't move my face because my skin was so badly burned and tight. The bus ride back home was 18 hours long. I reflected during this ride and said, "What was the purpose of this? Why did this happen again? I was just traumatized with the same thing last year?"

I didn't understand it, but there are no mistakes, and I did see the numbers 777. To my spiritual knowledge I went through a portal of evolution. Sometimes the spirit knows what the fleshly body doesn't. My finite mind struggled to comprehend this horrendous experience. However, when an energy exchange is made spiritually it takes a while to show up in the physical realm.

When I got home, I started crying and was unrecognizable. I had white stuff oozing out of my ears. My face was completely disfigured and needed to go through a healing process. I felt like a failure and like I was cursed. Every time there was a good moment in my life something bad kept happening.

One of my cousins got me the cream to get rid of my burns and scars. I was grateful to that because it was a huge help. The healing process was long, and I had horrible PTSD. I would have severe panic attacks and cry out of nowhere. I couldn't breathe when I was like this and some days, I felt like screaming. It was a fucking nightmare. All I would tell my mom is, "I can't take it anymore." All these back-to-back experiences were too much.

There were some songs that helped me cope through this process. I loved listening to Billie Eilish, *Everything I Wanted* because I had tried to commit suicide not too long before I heard this song. It helped my heart to heal. Another song that I loved although it was talking about some sort of initiation, was *Bury A Friend* by Billie Eilish. This helped me when I felt half dead and half awakened dealing with cancer.

Management had to refund me for the apartment because it wasn't finished, and I almost died there. The woman who worked in management had to be undiagnosed with some sort of mental illness because she was not sympathetic. I was glad to be out of that lease and get my funds back. Dealing with her was toxic.

Once my skin started to look a little bit more normal, I decided to focus on my career. Even though I was still extremely sick I was way too driven to escape that house. It wasn't supporting my mental, emotional, physical, or spiritual health. It was noisy there and I never had time to myself to breathe and be alone with my thoughts. I was aggravated all the time.

I decided to launch my Eat Stress Away Program but had no idea how to market it. I joined two different marketing guru groups. My mom had warned me not to join those groups, but I was so doubtful of who I was and my abilities. People had put me down so much and I felt beneath other people due to my living situation and my mental health issues that I was experiencing.

I reached out to a couple people, and they saw how great I was when I didn't see it. They decided to pluck at that and make condescending, belittling remarks. They knew I was sick and didn't care about how that would affect me. Their jealousy oozed out with the posts they put online and with their comments. I confronted one of them and she backpedaled, acting like she didn't say anything about me.

The other one I cussed out and told her she could meet me in person if she had an issue. I was fed up with their jealousy bullshit and wanted to projectile throw both of them towards steel, fucking wall. My membership with these social media FB ads people and these social media holistic hub people were short lived. So many people were putting me down during this time. How weak of those motherfuckers for coming at me during a low point? I came back ten times as hard and scared them away one by one.

I'm sure they thought I was crazy for calling their ass out, but I saw right through them because I'm naturally intuitive. Once I left those groups my Spirit connected me with likeminded individuals who saw my value and encouraged it. I stopped relying on people for marketing help and listened solely to my Spirit. The beginning of the growth of my spiritual medium and holistic health coaching business started when Creator, Spirit, Angels, ancient people, and more, awakened me.

They were giving me encouraging messages to boost my confidence and told me exactly what my purpose was. I was channeling messages from them for hours and I couldn't go to sleep. I recall when I started to go LIVE on my Facebook and Twitter. I would read my own cards that had essential oil and crystal names on them. I would see visions when I would read. However, people were not tuning in and weren't receptive to it, so I stopped doing it for a few months. The vibe was off.

. . .

I came back home at the right time because soon after I discovered there was a virus going around that was making people sick and afraid. I thought it was something that would come and go, but it lasted for a very long time. People were losing their jobs, people were dying, people were turning against each other because of the virus, and it was something out of a movie. If I had to relate this situation to any movies, they would be *Halloweentown* and *The Shelter* episode on *Twilight Zone*.

On the first *Halloweentown* people went from acting normal to being very angry, mean, and distraught. I saw people completely out of character during this time. It was atrocious. On *The Shelter* episode people were trying to invade this man's bomb shelter he built and didn't care about anyone else but themselves. In reality I saw people getting in fights over toilet paper, food, and people not wearing masks.

People were afraid that they wouldn't have the resources they needed to survive. The evilness that was displayed by people who wanted to force others to wear masks was uncalled for. I was shocked by their behavior and wanted no parts of that. During this time, I didn't leave the house at all. I was still recovering and didn't wear masks over my face with my condition so I couldn't go anywhere.

The only time I had to leave the house was to go see an oncologist. My holistic doctor wrote me a referral letter to see the oncologist at the local hospital. I got into an argument with my doctor who refused to write me a note stating that I couldn't wear a mask. I was infuriated because I struggled to breathe already and anything over my face would have suffocated. I thought to myself, "What the fuck is wrong with him?"

The hospital also wouldn't let me in the building without a facemask. The first time I went there I didn't wear a mask and they told me that next time I had to. I spoke to the oncologist, and we came to a compromise. He said, "I really want to find out what's wrong with you so could you wear the face mask when you enter the building and take it off in the room?" I was desperate at this point, so I agreed.

When it was time for my appointment, I wore the facemask and immediately started to suffocate so I pulled it off my face and held it with my hand. When I got in the room, I threw it away. They took my blood tests and flow cytometry tests. Prior to taking those tests the doctor also thought I had leukemia or lymphoma. When the results came back, I felt like throwing a shot putt Ms. Trunchbull style on *Matilda*.

It showed that I had Neutropenia and iron deficiency anemia, but nothing else. I started laughing, but it was because I was angry and frustrated. He contacted me shortly after and suggested I have a cat scan and bone marrow biopsy because he suspected I had cancer. However, I declined because I was tired of having my blood taken several times a week. I even had the blood test company contact me and ask how I was doing.

They felt empathy for me and wanted to make sure that I was okay. I stopped having all the test taken and stuck with my own diagnosis because it correlated with all the symptoms. I remember watching various YouTube videos on how people were diagnosed with leukemia or cancer.

. . .

The consensus amongst all of them was coughing and bruising. I had way more symptoms than that and couldn't get a solid diagnosis. My holistic doctor said I probably did have Mast Cell Leukemia, but due to the fact that I changed my diet since 2019 the tests came back normal. I was still mad, but I felt like I wasn't far off in my initial diagnosis.

There was nothing I could do at this point but to focus on getting better and my career. I would post my transformation pictures in Facebook groups because I was looking for clients and wanted to put myself out there. People were very engaging and interactive. However, the people in charge of each group I posted in got jealous and deleted my posts but kept other people's posts.

I did gain one client before I even launched my Eat Stress Away Program, which was encouraging. Other groups I joined were entrepreneurship groups that once again let other women promote their programs, but not me. I wish I was making this shit up, but I'm not. It happened repeatedly and was something I got used to. Eventually I left those groups due to feeling tolerated not celebrated. Before I left a woman in India contacted me.

She thought I would be a perfect fit for her global summit she was having. This invitation uplifted my spirits and I gladly agreed to participate. The summit was designed to encourage women to launch their online program. It was fun to be interviewed about my newly launched program and to be able to impart in other women's lives. After the summit was over, I got the opportunity to be in a book collaborating with women from all over the world. This book was created to motivate women to find their Why and discover their purpose.

I met with all these women during the summer of 2020 to discuss the book and details behind it. The book was released in August 2020 and became an international bestseller. I was ecstatic and felt like a phenomenal woman. Shortly after the book was released, I was asked to participate in another global summit and enjoyed myself as I spoke about what I was passionate about.

I went on to make connections with some of the women and did interviews with them on their platforms. It was a great experience and what I needed to stay motivated in my own career. In December 2020 I started to create TikTok videos. I started TikTok in 2019 and did short mukbang videos that weren't popular at all. It wasn't the right time. When I decided to come back to TikTok I talked about stress, anxiety, health, and did short mukbang videos.

I gained followers quickly, but those followers weren't turning into clients. I also didn't like talking about those topics all the time. Until this day I don't remember what prompted me or how I even got started to spiritual readings, channeled messages, and tarot readings on my TikTok. This became a hit with everyone. My videos started to go viral, and I was getting clients booking readings with me left and right.

I went from two followers to 14,000 followers in less than a year. This brings me back to some months before when the spirit realms awakened me, and they told me what my purpose was and who I was. I always had the gift of sight, but it was ignored. This gift was utilized in my own life. My mom and a couple aunts knew that I could see things. Sometimes my aunt would have me prophesy in Church and sometimes I would prophesy to her as well. This gift runs in my family.

All of my readings were spot on. Although I knew my capabilities it was still weird that everything was spot on. Throughout my life I was constantly warning people and sharing what I saw. Everything would come true, but I wasn't recognized as a psychic or prophetess. The spirit realms called me Vates, which means fortune-teller.

My business had picked up and this worked out perfectly for me because a few months after in March 2021 something happened at my uncle's house that caused a huge rift between him, my mom, and I. We were basically forced to move out. I was glad I was making funds enough to support myself and looked forward to being away from that environment.

I remember a couple weeks before this rift occurred, I was walking to CVS. I told myself, "I'm never getting out of here. I'm going to be stuck." As I walked past people shooting up drugs and down worn down streets I started to feel low in mood. Then I was reminded of when I went to look at a place at Manchester, Connecticut and how peaceful it was there.

I thought about the goals I wanted to accomplish if I was to move there. I also said, "In order to see change you must take action." This gave me the drive to start looking for places. When my mom and I were forced to move out while I was sick, I had one week to find a place. To my surprise I found a luxury apartment in a quiet suburb. This was a blessing in disguise. When evil is present only good can come afterwards. The apartment in Ohio circled back to my memory. One of the main reasons I regretted coming back to Hartford all the way from North Canton, Ohio was because of how quiet it was.

At Ohio my new hairdresser, the park and stores were in walking distance. The people were pleasant it was extremely quiet. I was happy when I stumbled across this brand-new apartment, and it was similar to what I experienced in Ohio. The apartments were also smoke free so there were no worries about me dying there.

I filled out an application using my unique identification and was approved. Everything had worked out for the better. One of my cousins brought my mom to put the down payment on this place while I was doing readings for a client. A relative helped us move to the new place and I felt free. My mom didn't want to move in with me but had to because it's hard to find places with certain identification.

If she didn't move in with me, she would have nowhere to go so we had to move together. I had to adjust to this new place, while suffering from PTSD from the other place. Although I had quiet time and freedom here, I was so used to scheduling in my time or delaying projects due to the noise and being around other people.

.   .   .

It took a while to get used to being free. My mom and I had our moments and things were volatile once again, but eventually died down. Both of us weren't proud of our actions. She dealt with her own PTSD after losing her mom, taking care of her mom, being in that toxic house, and having to take care of me while sick. I was dealing with PTSD after dealing with my sickness and similar things. None of us had time to breathe away from each other, but eventually came to a peaceful resolution. We don't see eye-to-eye all the time and had family interventions to mediate certain issues. People listened to both sides, but mainly took up for my mom so I don't have any interventions anymore because although I'm listened to, I'm never heard.

We both apologized verbally and through actions and decided to move on from the past volatile relationship we once had. I'm not ashamed of anything I've ever done. I accept the lessons and do my best not to repeat them. When I first moved in there was a new carpet smell and I thought, "I'm officially cursed and not meant to be happy ever. I'm a horrible person who did some fucked up shit in a past life and my karma is awful."

This was round four of me burning from the inside out. I broke out in petechiae, which is a leukemia rash, my skin started bruising, my face turned red, and I got some scaly patches again. I wanted to die because I thought my life was doomed and I was over it. I couldn't sleep and my cough was terrible. I cried as my nose was running and felt icky.

This time I stuck it out and diffused Eucalyptus and Breathe essential oil blend around the clock. I drank oregano, lemon, and Breathe essential oil water daily to boost my immune system. I used the OnGuard essential oil blend to boost my immune system. I bathed in essential oils and constantly drank water. I called my holistic doctor during this time, but he was mad at me over the mask ordeal and told me to find another doctor. I was shocked and thought to myself, "Wow a man acting like a bitch. What a little bitch?!"

Then I invested in a vacuum and put apple cider vinegar and baking soda on the carpet to get the smell out. After that I opened the windows as I was sleeping. It took one month to get rid of this and I didn't tell a soul. People wanted me to fail and not succeed in my new apartment, so I kept this to myself. I got online and even thought I shouldn't have worn makeup I did to cover my face as I did my online readings.

My focus was to get better, not fail, and get clients. Some tarot readers got jealous of my gifts on TikTok and wished me harm while I was sick. They didn't know I was recovering from cancer and had burned from the inside out, but they were still evil. I confronted the one who was trying to come for me, but she got scared. The karma she put towards me is what made me feel better. It reversed the sickness and I started to see my health improve.

My crystals, angels, spirit, and the Creator were very protective of me and weren't standing for anyone to come up against me because I was revealing their messages to help people. My readings consisted of health, stress, anxiety, and love. They were designed to help people, but not be sugarcoated.

· · ·

To this day I continue to help people and fulfill my purpose. My reading clients started to enroll in my programs and at my new apartment I created 4 new programs. My life's purpose is in the spiritual and holistic health field. I guide other people to their purpose and destiny through nutrition, lifestyle, and spirituality.

I'm grateful for my life because I know where I came from. I'm still growing in my business and as a person. My mental health has greatly improved. I've since healed from my abusive past and recent traumas. I no longer get depressed and have more of a positive outlook on life. If ever I feel down, I usually get to the root of it, refocus my attention on something that uplifts me, I meditate, workout, and read books that keep my mind occupied. Coming across a popular holistic doctor and naturopath who specializes in spirituality, nutrition, and medicine was a Godsend.

He was the one who confirmed that I did have cancer as well as kidney failure, pituitary issues, lymphatic system issues, adrenal dysfunction, and neurological issues, such as the ataxia I was experiencing. I finally felt like I was sane and as if I was heard. His herbs and tinctures helped me with my allergies, food sensitivities and problems. I'm still recovering from cancer, but I know I'm not going to die.

I have the tools to get better and know what I need to do to stay on track. If I can make it out, then you can do it as well.

PLACES

Places that I was were the Places that I went
The wait that made me a mental mess
The longing for the sunlight
Oh peace I wondered what that would taste like

This juxtaposed life that made me contemplate suicide multiple
times were a part of the corporate dance

The patriarchal mindset that revoked the same chance at living
my life freely a utopia where I could worship the greatest deity
and activate the power vested in me

I craved what my soul needed, but damnit those places I went.
Where was my mental sanity. How dare he, how dare she, how
dare they destroy my victory

To death lie the warrior in me
Begging for oxygen on bended knee
There it was the ultimate discovery

Whom the Sun sets free is free indeed
To unlock the key to spirituality
This day new life was breathed in me a heart attack that would
bring to life a new beginning

ABOUT THE AUTHOR

Avishai El is an international best-selling author of the Power of Why Book Series. She is an international, professional speaker, and host of the most blunt holistic health podcast, Avi Unfiltered. She is a Spiritual Medium and Holistic Health Coach who empowers people to fulfill their purpose and destiny on this planet. Teaching others the holistic lifestyle utilizing nutrition, lifestyle, and spiritual methods is her passion. Avishai has worked with women all over the world and has helped them lose weight, change their mental health for the better, develop businesses, and reverse several diseases. She has won an award for educating hundreds of people on the benefits of essential oils. Hospitals have entrusted her to be on hospital papers as a holistic nurse for cancer patients. People come to her when they are in a health crisis and Avishai has saved lives using holistic therapies. As an avid vegan she heavily promotes the plant-based, vegan lifestyle. The planet and Human Rights mean everything to her as she affirms everyone has the right to life, liberty, and the pursuit of happiness. She comes from ancient ancestry and is currently in the process of learning her native languages: Latin, Moorish Latin (Modern Day Spanish), Chaldean (Modern Day Hebrew), Arabic, and Amharic. Astrology and medical research on an array of topics geek her out, and is something she thoroughly enjoys studying. Black, white, and grey are her go-to colors and the minimalistic lifestyle brings her so much peace. She is multitalented and when she's not writing, speaking, coaching clients, or running her many businesses, she is doing some form of interior design, graphic design, honing in on her innate makeup skills, randomly playing violin, singing, doing comedy, and so much more.

ALSO BY AVISHAI EL

Earthly Desserts

Love Like Chocolate

Dark Chocolate Love